Assessing Student Learning in the School Library Media Center

Edited by

Anita L. Vance, MSLS

Assistant Editor,

Robbie Nickel, MSLS

Featuring contributions from the 2006 AASL Fall Forum particpants

AASL   **American Association of School Librarians**

The paper used in this publication meets the minimum requirements of American National Standards for Information Sciences—Permanence of Paper for Printed Library Materials, ANSI 239.481992.

ISBN 0-978-0-8389-8446-8

Published by:
American Association of School Librarians
a division of the American Library Association
50 E. Huron St.
Chicago, Illinois 60611-2795
To order, call 800-545-2433, press 7
<http://www.alastore.ala.org/aasl>

Table of Contents

Foreword

Anita L. Vance, Editor

The planning of the 2006 National Institute revolved around various concerns: What topic should be addressed? Where will the focus be in two years? How do we create a usable forum for all types of school librarians? What can we offer that will enhance the learning community on all levels? Where can we make the greatest impact?

The passing of No Child Left Behind legislation helped direct the response. The natural reaction across the nation included the location and implementation of full-scale assessment applications. Suddenly, the educational community was forced to present evaluative statistics regarding student achievement. In the scramble to find summative examinations and measurable results, the methods of learning and applying such concepts as information literacy have been overturned. Does that mean the testing process should usurp the teaching of such ethereal matters? Only if you wish to lose the influence we have gained in the real world of tangible research. Without finding the force or method of inclusion for the present educational prescriptive, we will be left behind in favor of automated, repetitive, regurgitated, and unconnected memorizations. Not that we need to jump on the "measure by testing" bandwagon. However, we *do* need to be part of a solution that balances memorization and practice with meaningful applications.

For instance, how does a student perform the correct algorithm unless the concrete connection for correct application takes place? Likewise, how does a student correctly create an informative or persuasive essay unless the original connection to effective writing elements has been made? Models and examples of excellent writing are plentiful in our school library media centers (SLMC). Process-oriented research methods are so much a part of successful thinking and writing that the credit for any success in these areas often bypasses the very center where the practice and application appear on a daily basis. Without the recognition of this process and practice connection, the SLMC is easily overlooked, left behind, or lost. Worse than that, the positive results of effective application are attributed to the Internet, Al Gore, Bill Gates, SpongeBob, or any number of celebrities.

Although identifying student progress connected to information fluency applied in the SLMC is a thought-provoking process, it must be done. This National Institute and its accompanying book have been prepared to present various methods and opportunities for all of us to understand and begin the identification, evaluation, and assessment of our students. The gathering of highly recognized experts for this effort includes: Vi Harada, who guided us through assessment processes within the school setting; Barbara Stripling, who definitively outlined the areas of possibility for varying methods of assessment; Judith Dzikowski, who located the backbone of test question formulation to assist in our collaborative discussions with the teaching community; Marjorie Pappas, who provided various methods and organizers for student assessment; and Allison Zmuda, who directed our methods for alignment with our purpose and ignited our passions that we might give our students their best opportunities for success.

The Fall Forum, which took place October 13–15, 2006, would not have been possible without the generous support of our sponsors: Walden Media, Libraries Unlimited, and Coughlan Publishing, which includes the imprints Capstone Press, Compass Point Books, Stone Arch, and Picture Window Books. More than five hundred enthusiastic participants confirmed our choice of topic and reaffirmed the need for information and support in this area.

The following pages summarize the forum offerings and include the welcoming statement from Cyndi Phillip, 2006–2007 AASL president, and Fall Forum chair Catherine Marriott; brief biographies of forum presenters and facilitators; articles based on keynote addresses and breakout sessions; and lists of questions generated by participants. Additional items include forum handouts, a glossary of assessment terms, bibliographies of cited sources, and a list of fiction titles about testing.

It is hoped that these resources will help school librarians become adept at documenting student progress, measuring student growth, and confirming the substantial impact of library media programs and centers on student learning.

Fall Forum 2006 Welcome

Welcome to the AASL Fall Forum, "Assessing Student Learning in the School Library Media Center." It is hard to believe that two years have elapsed since the Teaching for Learning Committee volunteered to plan the 2006 Fall Forum. The committee had been together as a task force until recently, when AASL elevated the task force to the Teaching for Learning Committee. As a group, we have conducted two ALA preconferences—one in Atlanta, Georgia, and one in Toronto, Canada—and prepared a *Knowledge Quest* issue on collaboration. We decided that we had the energy to tackle the Fall Forum, and AASL approved. In searching for a topic for the Fall Forum, we agreed that it needed to be a subject of national interest. Since the No Child Left Behind Act of 2001, reform measures in all of our schools challenge every member of the educational community to identify what students are learning and how well they are learning. If we envision our libraries as centers of active engagement and learning, what evidence do we have of our effectiveness beyond the number of books purchased and the resources circulated?

In considering what the school library media specialist's role is in assessing student learning, we have enlisted the talents of Violet Harada, professor of library and information science at the University of Hawaii and co-author of *Assessing Learning* (Libraries Unlimited, 2005). She will address why it is important to assess learning and why it should be our priority as teacher-librarians. Beyond information literacy (the ability to find and use information) is the ability to use information appropriately and effectively. An equally popular speaker, Barbara Stripling, past president of AASL and director of library media services for New York City, will lead us through the assessment of information fluency, a continuum of skills that extends beyond the K–12 environment.

After learning about the importance of assessment and what it might look like in various settings, we will have three breakout sessions, facilitated by featured speakers Violet Harada, Barbara Stripling, and Sharon Coatney, currently acquisitions editor of Libraries Unlimited and Teacher Ideas Press. Guided by Harada, Stripling, Coatney, and Teaching for Learning Committee members, participants will use the information learned and assessment's connection to the information literacy continuum to develop learning experiences. Linda Corey, Bonnie Grimble, Irene Kwidzinski, and practitioners will model the collaborative planning process, which will precede group identification of a lesson's learning target, performance task, and assessment tool. The results of this activity will be shared.

What would a library symposium be without literature? Enjoy a delicious lunch accompanied by a review of children's and young adult literature with an assessment theme.

After lunch, each group will be led through the process of standardized test question item analysis. The essential questions that will be answered are "What are the skills needed to answer standardized assessment questions?" and "What is the connection to the school library media?" Judith Dzikowski, Peter McCarthy, and Mary Tiedemann from the Onondaga-Cortland-Madison Counties Board of Cooperative Educational Services will facilitate a critical look at national assessments. Marjorie Pappas, writer, consultant, and virtual professor of library science, will follow this exercise, demonstrating assessment tools that can help school library media specialists tame the data. After a day of intense learning, lively discussion, and hard work, we will enjoy a networking reception.

The last day of the Fall Forum begins with Allison Zmuda, senior education specialist for the Capitol Regional Education Council (CREC) in Hartford, Connecticut, who will lead a provocative discussion on "Who Gives You the Authority to Do What You Are Doing?" She will give you the techniques to communicate to your faculty the library media center's potential to increase student achievement through collaboration and as a partner in student assessment.

The symposium will conclude with reflection and action planning. Vi Harada will facilitate the summarization of the learning that occurred at the Fall Forum with assistance from all participants.

The Teaching for Learning Committee extends our best wishes to all attendees for a productive and stimulating experience.

Catherine E. Marriott   Cynthia Phillip
Fall Forum Chair   AASL President

Forum Presenters and Facilitators

Sharon Coatney, Breakout Sessions I & II

After thirty years as a teacher and librarian, Sharon Coatney has "retired" to become an acquisitions editor for Libraries Unlimited and Teacher Ideas Press. Her publication credits include "Assessment in the School Library Media Center" in *Principles and Practice: Curriculum Connections through the Library* (Libraries Unlimited, 2003) and a list of other publications, including the Mac Information Detective series, a storybook approach to teaching information literacy skills to primary-age students (Libraries Unlimited). Coatney has been an adjunct professor for Ottawa, Baker, and Emporia universities in Kansas; co-chair of the Library Media Certification Standards Committee, National Board for Professional Teaching Standards; and an AASL president.

Judith A. Dzikowski, Item Analysis

Judith A. Dzikowski is the director of the Onondaga-Cortland-Madison Counties Board of Cooperative Educational Services School Library System and has thirty-three years of experience in the field of education as teacher, school library media specialist, and principal. Within AASL, she has participated as a member of the 2007 Nominating Committee and is the 2006 recipient of the AASL/Highsmith Research Grant. She also has served as the 2002 president of the New York School Library System Association. The Central New York Library Resources Council has benefited from Judith's commitment as a member of both the Board of Trustees (1998–2005) and Finance Committee (2003–2004).

Violet Harada, General Session: What Is Assessment and Why Should the School Librarian Be Involved?

Violet Harada publishes frequently in both scholarly and popular journals, and she has spoken at numerous state, national, and international conferences on the topic of libraries and learning. Along with Joan Yoshina, she co-authored *Assessing Learning: Librarians and Teachers as Partners* (Libraries Unlimited, 2005) and *Inquiry Learning: Through Librarian-Teacher Partnerships* (Linworth Publishing, 2004); her current research focuses on inquiry-based approaches to information seeking and use and on the dynamics of collaborative instruction and assessment. She is a past recipient of the AASL/Highsmith Research Grant and is presently one of the principal investigators on a $6 million National Science Foundation initiative, Hawaii Networked Learning Communities. Harada is professor of Library and Information Science at the University of Hawaii.

Marjorie L. Pappas, Session II: Assessment Tools

Marjorie Pappas is a writer, consultant, and virtual professor of library science. She is the co-author of Pathways to Knowledge, an information process mode, and *Pathways to Knowledge and Inquiry Learning* (Libraries Unlimited, 2002); additionally, she has written many articles on information literacy, inquiry learning, and virtual libraries. Pappas has been a library science professor at several universities; she presents frequently at state and national conferences.

Barbara Stripling, Session I: Assessing Information Fluency

Barbara Stripling has had a thirty-year career in education as a classroom teacher in Colorado and North Carolina, as a K—12 library media specialist in Arkansas, as a Library Power director in Tennessee, as a school district director of instructional services in Arkansas, and as director of library programs at New Visions for Public Schools, a local education fund in New York City. She is currently director of library services for the New York City Department of Education and has written or edited numerous books and articles, including her latest, *Curriculum Connections through the Library: Principles and Practice* (Libraries Unlimited, 2003). Stripling is a former AASL president and a former member of the ALA Executive Board.

Allison Zmuda, Session III: Who Gives You the Authority to Do What You Are Doing?

Allison Zmuda is a senior education specialist for the Capitol Regional Education Council in Hartford, Connecticut, where she works with staff to design curriculum, assessment, and instruction. A former high school social studies teacher, she transitioned to the role of educational consultant seven years ago and has co-authored *The Competent Classroom* (Teachers College Press and the National Education Association, 2001) and *High Stakes High School* (Simon and Schuster, 2001). Her latest book, *Transforming Schools: Creating a Culture of Continuous Improvement* (Association for Supervision and Curriculum Development, 2004), was the Association of Curriculum and Development April 2004 member book.

Teaching for Learning Committee Members

The responsibility of the design for the 2006 AASL Fall Forum was undertaken by the Teaching for Learning Committee.

Team I, National Institute Planning

Cathie Marriott, AASL Fall Forum Chair
Director of Technology and Information Services,
Orchard Park Central Schools
Orchard Park, New York

Debbie Abilock
Editor-in-Chief, *Knowledge Quest*
kq@abilock.net

Sharon Coatney (Team I and Team II)
Acquisitions Editor, School Library Media,
Libraries Unlimited

Linda Z. Cooper (Team I and Team II)
Associate Professor, Coordinator, LMS Program,
School of Information and Library Science,
Pratt Institute
New York, New York

Linda Kay Corey
District Coordinator, Blue Valley School District,
Overland Park, Kansas

Judith Dzikowski (Team I and Team II)
Director, OCM School Library System
Past President, School Library System Association
 (SLSA)
Syracuse, New York

Gail Formanack (Team I and Team II)
Supervisor of Library Services,
Omaha Public Schools
Omaha, Nebraska

Bonnie Grimble (Team I and Team II)
Media Specialist, Carmel High School
Indianapolis, Indiana

Karen Gavigan
Director, Teaching Resources Center,
University of North Carolina at Greensboro

Irene Kwidzinski (Team I and Team II)
AASL Director, Region 1, New England
Past President, New England Educational Media
 Association and the Connecticut Educational
 Media Association

Teaching for Learning Team II— National Institute Extensions

Anita L. Vance, Chair
Past President, Pennsylvania School Librarians'
 Association
Chestnut Ridge High School Librarian
Altoona, Pennsylvania

Audrey Church
Coordinator, School Library Media Program,
Longwood University
Farmville, Virginia

Kathleen Morrissey McBroom
Dearborn Public Schools
Dearborn, Michigan

Robbie Leah Nickel
Sage Elementary School
AASL Director-Elect, Region VII
President, Elko County Reading Council
Spring Creek, Nevada

Chapter 1 As assessment becomes the focus for school improvement and funding decisions, school library media specialists (SLMSs) need to expand their role as major contributors to this essential component of the learning process. Our impact on student learning is imbedded in activities and projects and is not easily measurable through paper-and-pencil testing. Much of what we teach involves the connection of ideas and information, providing the pathways to learning for each student. Often, it is a developmental process, with results that are difficult to measure. However, that does not remove us from the assessment process. Instead, it forces us to find new methods for measuring our student successes. Our assessments need to define the moment of information application and point out the effect of that moment on student learning. In this chapter, Vi Harada reveals opportunities for the SLMS to guide assessment through genuine learning experiences. Harada then offers insight into the learning process, following students through discovery, research, assimilation, rediscovery, further research, evaluation, and other lesson extensions that occur on the way to a final product.

Assessing Student Learning

Why Should Library Media Specialists Be Involved?

Author's Note: This article is based on a keynote address delivered at the 2006 Fall Forum sponsored by the American Association of School Librarians in Providence, Rhode Island.

As school library media specialists (SLMSs), we teach an average of more than six hundred lessons a year. We spend at least three hours of preparation each time that we create new lessons. In any school, we are among the few professionals on campus who service the entire student and faculty populations. In short, we are dedicated teachers. The question is: how do we know how well our students are actually learning?

When I informally polled my colleagues in the field about this matter of assessing student learning, I repeatedly received the following responses: "I eyeball the room while students are working in the library"; "I spot check students' work as I circulate"; "If I do a lesson on resources for research, I check the number and types of books borrowed"; "I look for that glimmer of discovery when the light bulb goes on in a student's head."

As busy professionals, informal assessment, or "assessment on the fly," is certainly a valuable and pragmatic strategy; however, it falls short of providing confirming evidence of actual learning. When we eyeball the room or spot-check students' work, we get a gross sense of how students are managing, but we don't capture data on the individual student's progress. Circulation statistics might give us an indication of what students are borrowing, but they do not help us understand what the students are actually doing with the resources. While glimmers of discovery are exciting to observe, we must discover ways to document these "a-ha" moments. The bottom line is that we must implement methods for assessing student learning that are measurable and informative.

Violet H. Harada

Professor, Library and Information Science Program, Department of Information and Computer Sciences, University of Hawaii

Defining Assessment

Assessment is the process of collecting, analyzing, and reporting data that informs us about progress and problems that a student encounters in a learning experience (Harada and Yoshina 2005; Coatney 2003). Derived from the Latin word *assidere,* assessment involves mentors talking with and working alongside learners (Donham 1998).

Assessment serves many purposes, including assessment of learning, assessment for learning, and assessment for advocacy. I briefly describe these three purposes below and elaborate more deeply on assessment for learning and assessment for advocacy as key themes for our consideration.

Assessment of Learning

Assessment of learning is what we traditionally refer to as *evaluation.* It is summative and judgmental in nature (Harada and Yoshina 2005; Asp 1998). Because we associate assessment of learning with grading, the instructor is largely responsible for evaluation. In education, we use summative assessment for programmatic and system accountability; for example, administering unit examinations, determining the effectiveness of a new curriculum program, or judging the performance of students on statewide, norm-referenced tests.

Assessment for Learning

Assessment for learning, on the other hand, is ongoing and formative rather than summative. It emphasizes thoughtful reflection and not evaluative judgment; therefore, the learner is centrally involved in the process (Donham 1998). Students ask themselves, "Where am I going?" "Where am I now?" "How do I close the gap?" (Stiggins 2005; Cross 1999).

When instructors use assessment measures prior to a learning experience, such as for pre-assessment, the data helps them shape this experience. Research confirms that this form of assessment sharpens the instructors' ability to modify instruction (Stiggins 2002; Earl 2003; Marzano 2003). It enables them to provide specific and personalized feedback to individuals and teams and allows for teaching that differentiates expectations and tasks for students based on assessment data (Chappuis and Stiggins 2002).

Students and teachers use a wide range of tools and strategies to assess performance. These instruments range from learning logs and constructed responses to rating scales and rubrics (Andrade 2000). They also may design graphic organizers (such as K-W-L charts, concept maps, Venn diagrams, T-charts) that capture different learning objectives (Harada and Yoshina 2005; Harada and Yoshina 2006; Strickland and Strickland 2000; Davies 2000; Pappas 1997).

Assessment for learning also is a communal endeavor. Along with the student and classroom teacher, other mentors can be central partners in examining students' progress. SLMSs are key team members along with other potential teaching partners, including technology coordinators, resource teachers, and community experts (Davies et al. 1992).

Examples of Library Involvement in Assessment for Learning

In this segment, I describe three scenarios based on actual practices in an elementary, middle, and high school setting.

Scenario 1: Pacific Elementary School

The context. A group of kindergartners discovered a strange insect on the school playground during recess. Their teacher captured the insect in a jar and used this teachable moment to introduce inquiry learning. All the students wanted to know the identity of this bug and whether or not it was poisonous. When three students volunteered to find out more about the bug, the teacher involved the SLMS in the investigation. Unfortunately, the "bug detectives" were unable to find details about their insect among the library resources, so the SLMS helped them draft the following e-mail message to an entomologist at the local university:

> We fownd a bug on the sidwok at or school. It is red and black. It has 2 antena and small sqares on the back. Kan you hlp us? We want to no if this bug is dangris and if it pichas and what it can do. Can you tell us its name too?

The entomologist responded the next day with the information that this was an assassin bug that used its long pinchers to skewer its prey and suck out their fluids for food. While it was not poisonous, the assassin bug might pinch, so he urged the students to warn others to avoid playing with the insect. The excited students decided that the information had to be shared with the rest of the school. As a class, they created posters of the insect to display around the campus. In addition, the three student detectives worked with the SLMS and the technology coordinator to create a one-minute video that was aired over closed-circuit television. The entire project took approximately a month of intermittent activity.

Assessment focus. The teacher and SLMS wanted to assess how well kindergartners were able to identify aspects of the inquiry process (Harada, Lum, and Souza 2002–2003). They decided to use simple class charts to capture prior knowledge (pre-assessment) and new knowledge gained (post-assessment).

Figure 1 reflects what the youngsters knew about the inquiry process before they undertook this project. Figure 2 captures what the students were able to articulate as a class following their investigation.

By creating these two artifacts, the instructors and students were able to compare and contrast the youngsters' prior and new knowledge about the inquiry process. In the pre-assessment chart, the students understood the importance of questions driving the search for information. In the post-assessment chart, we see that students were able to verbalize other critical aspects of the process, including the need to tap prior knowledge,

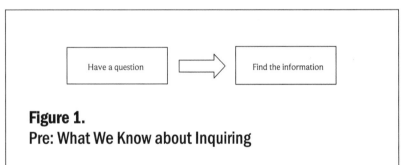

Figure 1.
Pre: What We Know about Inquiring

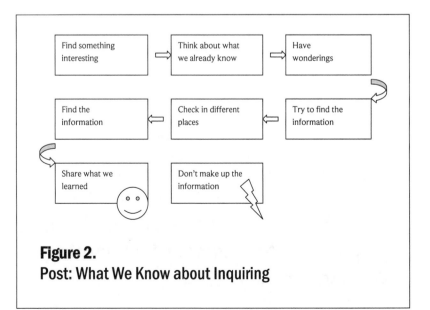

Figure 2.
Post: What We Know about Inquiring

search in more than one place for information, and share the learning with others. In addition, they realized the ethical responsibility to produce accurate information.

Scenario 2: Island Middle School

The context. The sixth graders in a social studies class engaged in two cycles of research. In the first cycle, which lasted nearly eight weeks, they focused on the overarching question: Are ancient civilizations still alive today? How do we know? They created artifacts (such as miniature replicas, dioramas, posters) to display in the schoolwide Curriculum Fair, which was attended by parents and community members.

In the second cycle, which lasted for four weeks, the students tackled the following questions: "What makes a hero?" "Who would I choose as a hero from history?" "Why?" They created posters that they mounted in a Hall of Fame of Historical Heroes in the school cafetorium for Parents' Night.

Assessment focus. The teacher and SLMS assessed students' ability to identify important aspects of the information search process (Harada 2002). For this purpose, students maintained biweekly electronic logs during their two cycles of research. By maintaining these logs electronically, students were able to compare logs written during the first cycle with those composed during the second cycle. Both the teacher and the SLMS collaborated on responding to the logs. They used the same log prompts during both cycles so that they could compare students' responses for the two assignments.

Figure 3 is a student's log to the following prompt in the first cycle: If a new student came to our class, how would you explain the steps you would take to work on your research assignment? Figure 4 is the same student's log entry to a similar prompt in the second cycle.

In a conference with Gloria and her parents, the teacher and SLMS encouraged the student to compare her second entry with the earlier one. This allowed the student to reflect on what she had learned about the information search process and to share this assessment with her parents. She acknowledged that at the beginning of her first research project, she thought that getting a topic was sufficient and that one resource, the electronic

---

"I would tell her to find a topic and go to the library and use the electronic encyclopedia to find information. Then write it up and turn it in."

Figure 3.
Gloria's Log: Cycle One

"You choose a broad topic. You might ask your teacher what you should write your report on, or what she requires you to do. To get a general picture, look through different resources. See if the resources are understandable. Select the best topic. Choose the topic that you think most people would not pick because teachers don't always want students to have the same things and also you could teach others something they might not have known. Make who, what, when, where, why and how questions. Find resources, scan through them. Use as many different resources as possible. Take notes by writing key words and long answers. *Don't copy your answers out of a book because the teacher knows what kind of work you do.* Now you are ready to put it into paragraphs. Put the info together so that *it makes sense.* Use correct grammar and check over your work. Finally you show others what you learned. Always assess your work. Be truthful. If you assess untruthfully, you will only be fooling yourself. In conclusion, doing a project is very time consuming and it takes patience. It takes dedication. Each time you do a project it should get better and better. Never TRY to do your best; just DO your best."

Figure 4.
Gloria's Log: Cycle Two

encyclopedia, would adequately satisfy the research assignment. Working on her second project, however, Gloria realized that

> there was much more to doing a good job. You really have to think seriously about the topic and the questions you want to ask. You can't find all of the information in any one source, and you can't just patch your notes together. You have to organize what you know so that other people will understand you.

Scenario 3: Paradise High School

The context. In a semester-long project, tenth-grade students in a language arts class wanted to focus their writing on a topic that was current and relevant. They voted to study the issues related to global pollution. Their questions focused on what factors affected global pollution, how bad the situation is, and what they can do about it. They ultimately created multimedia presentations to showcase their findings at a mock global summit sponsored by the local department of education. Members of the community were invited as responders at the summit.

Assessment focus. In this instance, the teacher had a number of content-specific learning goals. The two SLMSs focused on information-fluency skills, including students' ability to intelligently evaluate the usefulness of different Web sites. Working with the students, they identified three major criteria for evaluation: accuracy of the content, authority, and ease of use. The SLMSs devised a graphic organizer to evaluate the Web sites, and the students used the organizer to evaluate three Web sites at three different points in their search process. Because the teacher wanted to incorporate the results of the students' Web evaluations in her comprehensive scoring for the project, the SLMSs also devised a four-level proficiency scale to assess the students' work (see figure 5).

In addition, the SLMSs used a spreadsheet to record students' levels of proficiency for the three Web site evaluations and converted the results into a bar graph depicting the overall results for the class (see figure 6).

Level 4   I can accurately evaluate the Web site on all three of the criteria. I can provide supporting data.

Level 3   I can accurately evaluate the Web site on two of the three criteria. I can provide supporting data.

Level 2   I can accurately evaluate the Web site on one of the three criteria. I can provide supporting data.

Level 1   I have difficulty evaluating the Web site on all of the criteria.

Figure 5.
Levels of Proficiency

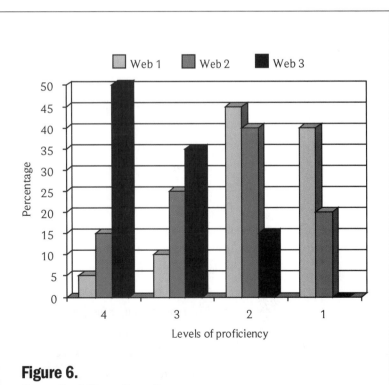

Figure 6.
Compiled Class Results

By studying the bar graph, both the students and teacher could see the improvements over time. For example, while only 5 percent of the students were functioning at Level 4 in the first evaluation, more than 50 percent were achieving that level by the third evaluation. In addition, 40 percent of the students were at Level 1 at the beginning, and none were at that level by the end. The results also were shared with the principal, who was impressed to see the evidence.

Assessment for Advocacy

Unlike assessing for learning, assessment for advocacy focuses on communicating evidence to the stakeholders and decision-makers in the school community who manage budgets and resources. These individuals are not interested in the individual student's progress; they are concerned about overall evidence of student achievements (Todd 2003). This focus for assessment, therefore, requires a strategic and selective approach to assessment (Harada and Yoshina 2006; Wiggins 1998; Wiggins and McTighe 1998).

As reported in *Teacher Librarian* (Harada 2005), a strategic approach to assessment involves the following steps:

- *Determine school goals and priorities.* This is a crucial first step. It is not about defending what the SLMS views as important, but what the decision-makers identify as critical for the school.
- *Determine the library's contribution to the goals.* Being strategic means examining the many tasks we perform and asking ourselves the crucial question "Which tasks directly align with the school's priorities?" By carefully identifying the major direction of the school program, we also decide where to channel our time and resources. By doing this, we emphasize the value-added nature of what we offer.
- *Identify specific learning targets.* We teach a wide spectrum of skills in our respective information literacy programs. Because we work with entire school populations, it would be impossible for us to formally assess every lesson taught. We need to be selective. Questions that help us make workable decisions include "Which learning targets are most directly related to the school's goals?" "How do the library's targets match the classroom's learning goals?" and "Which classes or grade levels might be most willing to collaborate with the library?" The aim is to narrow our targets and work with a manageable cohort of teachers. We want to establish reasonable boundaries so that we are not overwhelmed with the assessment tasks.
- *Establish criteria to measure student achievement of the learning targets.* In assessment-focused instruction, we start with an idea of what the students must be able to do at the end of the learning experience. This outcome-based approach to instructional planning is critical because it focuses our attention on what is essential for students to learn. The assessment criteria should be stated so that they are understandable not only to the instructors but to the students.
- *Devise assessment tools.* As mentioned earlier, a range of techniques and instruments might be used, including rubrics, rating scales, checklists, and logs. Whichever tool is used, the criteria must be clearly stated so that both students and instructional teams can apply them to determine levels of achievement.
- *Collect and analyze the data.* By systematically collecting the data and figuring ways to summarize and analyze the information, we can use the results to drive improvements in learning and teaching. As I described in the Paradise High School scenario, a useful technique is to enter the data on a spreadsheet. This allows us multiple options in terms of formatting, sorting, calculating, and presenting the results.

- *Communicate the results to different stakeholder groups.* The same assessment data can be packaged and presented in formats appropriate for different stakeholder groups, such as students, teachers, parents, and administrators. With students and parents, the critical focus is the individual student's progress and accomplishments. Instructional partners need the same student-by-student accounting; at the same time, they also require class profiles of this information. Administrators, however, desire broader summaries, where the data might be aggregated by grade levels or courses.

Example of Library Involvement in Assessment for Advocacy

SLMSs in Hawaii have seized this challenge by the horns (Harada 2006). Twenty-four K–12 SLMSs are voluntarily participating in a year-long professional development program titled "School Librarians Help Students Achieve: Here's the Evidence!" The project is a collaborative venture involving the Hawaii Association of School Librarians, the University of Hawaii's Library and Information Science Program, and the Hawaii State Department of Education's School Library Services. The intended outcome is to have SLMSs develop evidence folders to communicate what their students have achieved through library instruction. The audience for the folder is the stakeholder community, including administrators, faculty, and school community councils. The folder can be a paper or an online document (Harada 2006).

The core of the evidence folder is the synthesis and analysis of student learning that results from library instruction. The SLMSs in Hawaii realize that they cannot formally assess all of the lessons they teach; therefore, they are employing a strategic tactic to assessment. They began by asking themselves, "What are the most critical learning gaps that my students are facing at this time?" and "How does my teaching support the classroom teachers' efforts to close the gaps?" These questions have been essential ones, because they have forced the SLMSs to consider the value of what they teach from the perspective of the classroom.

In building their evidence folders, the Hawaii SLMSs have agreed on the following components as essential:

- brief description of how the library's mission connects with the school's mission;
- brief description of school's major learning targets for the school year;
- brief description of how instruction in the library connects with school's learning targets;
- samples of lessons taught in the library that connect with the school's learning targets;
- samples of student performance for each lesson in the folder;
- displays of compiled assessment data that communicate what students learned from these lessons;
- sample commentary from students about possible future improvements; and
- sample commentary from instructors about possible teaching improvements.

Conclusion

Ultimately, the purposes for assessment described in this article center on several critical questions that we must ask ourselves:

- What do we teach? Why is it important?
- Does our teaching make a difference? How do we know this?
- How do others know this?

The fundamental issues underlying the above questions deal with the value of the library media center and evidence of that value in terms of student learning. To state this bluntly, are we invisible, or are we visible and indispensable teaching partners? Do we view assessment as intuitive and incidental, or integral and intentional to learning? Do we simply spout the rhetoric on the importance of assessment, or can we demonstrate results? Each of us holds the power and the authority to close the learning gaps in our schools (Zamuda 2006). This is a challenge we cannot afford to ignore.

Works Cited

Andrade, H. G. 2000. "Using rubrics to Promote Thinking and Learning." *Educational Leadership* 57, no. 5: 13–18.

Asp, E. 1998. "The Relationship between Large-scale and Classroom Assessment: Compatibility or Conflict?" In *Assessing Student Learning: New Rules, New Realities,* 17–46, ed. R. Brandt. Arlington, Va.: Educational Research Service.

Chappuis, J., and R. J. Stiggins. 2002. "Classroom Assessment for Learning." *Educational Leadership* 60, no. 1): 40–43.

Coatney, S. 2003. "Assessment for Learning." In *Curriculum connections through the library,* 157–68, ed. B. K. Stripling and S. Hughes-Hassell. Westport, Conn.: Libraries Unlimited.

Cross, K. P. 1999. *Learning Is about Making Connections.* Princeton, N.J.: Educational Testing Service.

Davies, A. 2000. *Making Classroom Assessment Work.* Courtenay, B.C.: Connections Publ.

Davies, A., et al. 1992. *Together Is Better: Collaborative Assessment, Evaluation, and Reporting.* Winnipeg: Portage and Main Pr., 1992

Donham, J. 1998. *Assessment of Information Processes and Products.* McHenry, Ill.: Follett Software Co.

Earl, L. M. 2003. *Assessment As Learning: Using Classroom Assessment to Maximize Student Learning.* Thousand Oaks, Calif: Corwin Pr.

Harada, V. H. 2002. "Personalizing the Information Search Process: A Case Study of Journal Writing with Elementary-age Students." *School Library Media Research* 5. <http://www.ala.org/ala/aasl/aaslpubsandjournals/slmrb/slmrcontents/volume52002/harada.htm> (accessed 5 Jan. 2007).

Harada, V. H. 2005. "Working Smarter: Being Strategic about Assessment and Accountability." *Teacher Librarian* 33, no. 1: 8–15.

Harada, V. H. 2006. "Building evidence folders for learning through library media centers." *School Library Media Activities Monthly* 23, no. 3: 25–30.

Harada, V. H., D. Lum, and K. Souza. 2002/2003. "Building a learning community: Students and adults as inquirers." *Childhood Education* 79, no. 2: 66–71.

Harada, V. H., and J. M. Yoshina. 2005. *Assessing learning: Librarians and Teachers As Partners.* Westport, Conn.: Libraries Unlimited.

Harada, V. H., and J. M. Yoshina. 2006. "Assessing Learning: The Missing Piece in Instruction?" *School Library Media Activities Monthly* 22, no. 7: 20–23.

Marzano, R. J. 2003. *What Works in Schools: Translating Research into Action.* Alexandria, Va.: Association for Supervision and Curriculum Development.

Pappas, M. 1997. "Organizing research." *School Library Media Activities Monthly* 14, no. 4: 30–32.

Stiggins, R. J. 2002. "The Assessment Crisis: The Absence of Assessment FOR Learning." *Phi Delta Kappan* 83, no. 10: 758–65.

Stiggins, R. J. 2005. *Student-involved Assessment for Learning,* 4th ed. Upper Saddle River, N.J.: Pearson/ Merrill Prentice Hall.

Strickland, K., and J. Strickland. 2000. *Making Assessment Elementary.* Portsmouth, N.H.: Heinemann.

Todd, R. J. 2003. "School Libraries Evidence: Seize the Day, Begin the Future." *Library Media Connection* 22, no. 1: 12–17.

Wiggins, G. 1998. *Educative Assessment: Designing Assessments to Inform and Improve Student Performance.* San Francisco: Jossey-Bass.

Wiggins, G., and J. McTighe. 1998. *Understanding by Design.* Alexandria, Va.: Association for Supervision and Curriculum Development.

Zamuda, A. 2006. "Where Does Your Authority Come from? Empowering the Library Media Specialist As a True Partner in Student Achievement." *School Library Media Activities Monthly* 23, no. 1: 19–22.

Additional Resources

American Association of School Librarians and Association for Educational Communications and Technology. 1998. *Information Power: Building Partnerships for Learning.* Chicago: ALA.

Black, P., and D. William. 1998. "Inside the Black Box: Raising Standards through Assessment." *Phi Delta Kappan* 80, no. 2: 139–47.

Cawelti, G., ed. 2004. *Handbook of Research on Improving Student Achievement,* 3d ed. Arlington, Va.: Educational Research Service.

Dembo, M. H., and M. J. Eaton. 2000. "Self-regulation of Academic Learning in Middle-level Schools." *The Elementary School Journal* 100, no. 5: 473–90.

Dickinson, G. 2005. "How One Child Learns: The Teacher-librarian As Evidence-based Practitioner." *Teacher Librarian* 33, no. 1: 16–20.

Ekhaml, L. 1998. "Graphic organizers: Outlets for your thoughts." *School Library Media Activities Monthly* 14, no. 5: 29–33.

Falk, B. 2000. *The Heart of the Matter: Using Standards and Assessment to Learn.* Portsmouth, N.H.: Heinemann.

Gordon, C. 2000. "The effects of concept mapping on the searching behavior of tenth-grade students." *School Library Media Research* 3 <http://www.ala.org/ala/aasl/aaslpubsandjournals/slmrb/ slmrcontents/volume32000/mapping.htm> (accessed 4 Jan. 2007).

Gusky, T. R. 2003. "How Classroom Assessments Improve Learning." *Educational Leadership* 60, no. 5: 6–11.

Hawley, W. D., and D. I. Rollie. 2002. *The Keys to Effective Schools: Educational Reform As Continuous Improvement.* Thousand Oaks, Calif.: Corwin Pr.

Herman, J. L., P. R. Aschbacker, and L. Winters. 1992. *A Practical Guide to Alternative Assessment.* Alexandria, Va.: Association for Supervision and Curriculum Development.

Kuhlthau, C. C., ed. 1993. *Assessment and the School Library Media Center.* Englewood, Colo.: Libraries Unlimited.

Kuhlthau, C. C. 1993. *Seeking Meaning: A Process Approach to Library and Information Services.* Norwood, N.J.: Ablex.

Linn, R. L. 1991. "Complex Performance-based Assessment: Expectations and Validation Criteria." *Educational Researcher* 20, no. 8: 15–21.

Loertscher, D. V., and B. Woolls, eds. 2002. *Information Literacy: A Review of the Research,* 2d ed. San Jose, Calif.: Hi Willow.

Loertscher, D. V., with R. Todd. 2003. *We Boost Achievement! Evidence-based Practice for School Library Media Centers.* Salt Lake City: Hi Willow.

Marzano, R. J., D. Pickering, and J. McTighe. 1993. *Assessing Student Outcomes: Performance Assessment Using the Dimensions of Learning Model.* Alexandria, Va.: Association for Supervision and Curriculum Development.

Neuman, D. 2000. "Information Power and Assessment: The Other Side of the Standards Coin." In *Educational Media and Technology Yearbook,* 110–19, ed. R. M. Branch and M. A. Fitzgerald. Englewood, Colo.: Libraries Unlimited.

Newell, T. S. 2004. "Thinking beyond the disjunctive opposition of information literacy assessment in theory and practice." *School Library Media Research* 7. <http://www.ala.org/ala/aasl/aaslpubsandjournals/slmrb/slmrcontents/volume72004/beyond.htm> (accessed 4 Jan. 2007).

North Central Regional Educational Laboratory. n.d. "21st Century Skills." <http://www.ncrel.org/engauge/skills/agelit.htm> (accessed 4 Jan. 2007).

Northwest Regional Educational Laboratory. 2001. "Assessment Home-toolkit 98." <http://www.nwrel.org/assessment/toolkit98.php> (accessed 4 Jan. 2007).

Schrock, K. 2006. *Kathy Schrock's Guide for Educators: Assessment and Rubric Information.* <http://school.discovery.com/schrockguide/assess.html> (accessed 4 Jan. 2007).

Stefl-Mabry, J. 2004. "Building Rubrics into Powerful Learning Assessment Tools." *Knowledge Quest* 32, no. 5: 21–25.

Stripling, B. K. 1999. "Expectations for Achievement and Performance: Assessing Student Skills." *NASSP Bulletin* 83, no. 605: 44–52.

Todd, R. J. 2002. "Evidence-based Practice: The Sustainable Future for Teacher-librarians." *SCAN* 21, no. 1: 30–37. <http://www.schools.nsw.edu.au/schoollibraries/scan/researchfeature.htm> (accessed 4 Jan. 2007).

Todd, R. J. 2002. "Evidence-based Practice II: Getting into the Action." *SCAN* 21, no. 2: 34–41. <http://www.schools.nsw.edu.au/schoollibraries/scan/researchfeature.htm> (accessed 4 Jan. 2007).

University of Kansas Center for Research on Learning. 2006. "Rubistar: Create Rubrics for Your Project-based Learning Activities." <http://rubistar.4teachers.org/index.php> (accessed 4 Jan. 2007).

University of Wisconsin–Stout. 2006. "Rubrics: Teacher created rubrics for assessment." <http://www.uwstout.edu/soe/profdev/rubrics.shtml> (accessed 4 Jan. 2007).

William, D., et al. 2004. "Teachers Developing Assessment for Learning: Impact on Student Achievement." *Assessment in Education: Principles, Policy, and Practice* 11, no. 1: 49–65.

Wiske, M. S. 1994. "How teaching for understanding changes the rules in the classroom." *Educational Leadership* 51, no. 5: 19–21.

Voices of the Participants: Assessment—Why?

During the Fall Forum, audience members were asked to submit questions for evaluations and for inclusion in a continuing discussion via a newly developed ALA online community. Included here are some of the most significant questions posed by the national institute participants, with answers generated by the Teaching for Learning Committee.

How can we convince teachers "planning" is such a big part—if not the biggest part—of the collaborative process?

The argument for teacher participation in the planning process works best if the school library media specialist can propose a link to real world situations. "The closer the context can be to real-world situations, the more likely it is that students will see the connection between academic context and practical applications."—*Daniel Callison and Leslie Preddy,* The Blue Book on Information Age Inquiry, Instruction, and Literacy. *Westport, Conn.: Libraries Unlimited, 2006*

Once you have assessed the class, what do you do with the assessment? How can you improve?

Understanding that any assessment must have a target; for example, "The student will correctly identify the correct resource . . ." The level of achievement toward that goal or target, such as number of students choosing the correct resource, identifies the success of the instruction. If fewer than 80 percent of the class made the correct selection, a simple review of resource purpose could take the number to 90 percent. The time and place of the review would be determined by collaborative discussions with the cooperating teacher.—*Anita L. Vance, 2007 Teaching for Learning chair*

How do you lead teachers to realize they *can* teach content through project-based learning?

"The library media program provides a foundation for lifelong learning by combining effective learning and teaching strategies and activities with information access skills."—*American Association of School Librarians, ix*

The realization that best practices indicate the strength of the real-world connection, identifying natural connections included in the various curricula, becomes the first step towards guiding teachers to project-based assignments. A number of Web sites exist to help with that connection, among them <http://www.schools.nsw.edu.au/schoollibraries/scan/researchfeature.htm>; <http://www.statelibrary.state.pa.us/libraries/lib/libraries/Tool_Kit_Rev.pdf>; <http://rubistar.4teachers.org/index.php>; and <http://edsitement.neh.gov>.—*Anita L. Vance, 2007 Teaching for Learning chair*

Are we going to see testing of literacy skills embedded in content skills? Are these skills going to be measured as in state tests?

In the Pennsylvania School Librarians Association, discussion has centered on that very question. Presently, many states are dependent upon the testing companies, such as Educational

Testing Service (ETS), that use textbook sources and staff to create questions. A recent article on CNN.com states, "The NCLB testing industry is dominated by four companies: Harcourt of San Antonio, Texas; CTB/McGraw-Hill based in Monterey, California; Pearson Educational Measurement of Iowa City, Iowa; and Riverside Publishing of Itasca, Illinois" <http://www.cnn.com/2007/EDUCATION/03/25/nclb.standardized.test.ap/index.html>.

In those instances, writing to the company would be the only way to influence test questions. In other states, such as Ohio, where some tests are created by the Department of Education, librarian volunteers could help with content analysis and application. However, in the absence of clear lines of effect, item analysis, the strategy outlined by Judith A. Dzikowski during this national institute, would seem to be the most workable solution for SLMSs.—*Anita L. Vance, 2007 Teaching for Learning chair*

Because individual states develop their own tests, this will vary from state to state.

Literacy skills of all types (reading literacy, media literacy, information literacy, and so on) should be embedded in content area tests. In Virginia, these skills already are embedded, as can be seen by examining the state's Standards of Learning Blueprints <http://www.pen.k12.va.us/VDOE/Assessment/soltests> and the Released Test Items <http://www.doe.virginia.gov/VDOE/Assessment/releasedtests.html>.

It is imperative that SLMSs have access to standardized test data in the areas related to literacy. This allows us to target our instruction and then to measure its effectiveness.

A good article to read on this topic is M. Eisenberg's "It's All about Learning: Ensuring That Students Are Effective Users of Information on Standardized Tests," *Library Media Connection* 22, no. 6 (Mar. 2004): 22–30.—*Audrey Church, 2007 Teaching for Learning member*

How can we assess for transfer?

The very fact that we build curriculum as a continuum testifies that we expect transfer. Creating charts as simple as the Harada figures in this chapter gives some framework for pre-teaching and post-evaluations. The thinking for identification of skills could begin here.—*Anita L. Vance, 2007 Teaching for Learning chair*

How can we assess retainment?

Once again, our curriculum builds on the concepts presented before. The amount of review needed before a student successfully applies effective strategies is a general guideline. The pre- and post-teaching rubric is easily transferred here, as well.—*Anita L. Vance, 2007 Teaching for Learning chair*

How do our assessments suggest meaningful learning experiences?

By tying the measure of progress to a recognizable result, as exemplified by Vi Harada's journal entries, the meaningful learning experience becomes easily verifiable. Your efforts to collect such evidence need not be necessary for every nuance of research, but it should be part of collaborative discussions as targets and goals are set. Your own portfolio of best practices should contain examples of these types of connections.—*Anita L. Vance, 2007 Teaching for Learning chair*

What *are* the information skills we are trying to teach at the middle school level? How do we scaffold these skills from sixth to eighth grade?

Henrico County (Va.) Public Schools has developed an excellent scope and sequence of library information skills for grades K–12 as part of their Essentials of the Curriculum <http://www.henrico.k12.va.us/curriculum/library.html>.

Scaffolding is critical as students move from grade level to grade level, whether it is in elementary, middle, or high school. Having a scope and sequence for the library information skills curriculum provides the framework. Scaffolding is accomplished as library media specialists partner with classroom teachers to teach appropriate information skills in the context of the content area curriculum and as these learning opportunities are carefully and consistently planned and implemented at each grade level.—*Audrey Church, 2007 Teaching for Learning member*

Generally speaking, sixth-grade students are expected to correctly identify specific resource applications, such as almanacs for statistics and atlases for maps. At this level, they should also understand the purpose of the index and glossary, and so on. As they progress in research activities, the successful inclusion of these skills into project development, along with a component that indicates synthesis, provides the vehicle for scaffolding.

Specific examples can be found throughout several states where a library science or information literacy curriculum is available online. In Pennsylvania, for example, the Web page <http://www.statelibrary.state.pa.us/libraries/lib/libraries/Tool_Kit_Rev.pdf> offers different grade level applications as well as collaborative tools for use with faculty for planning.—*Anita L. Vance, 2007 Teaching for Learning chair*

How do we help/nudge the classroom teachers to value the process of information literacy/fluency more than the product?

"Success depends on three things: who says it, what he says, how he says it; and of the three things, what he says is the least important."—*John, Viscount Morley of Blackburn*

By identifying the most proactive teacher and building a successful project with him or her, the possibility of influencing others to participate becomes assured. That process, in and of itself, is your strongest building block.—*Anita L. Vance, 2007 Teaching for Learning chair*

This is difficult, and I'm not sure that we'll ever help, nudge, and move them *all* to this realization. They tend to be focused on their content, their discipline, and their products because (1) this is what is important to them, (2) this is primarily what their students are measured on during standardized testing, and (3) for the most part, this is the educational paradigm in which *they* learned.

I believe that we can *help* move them in the direction of this realization by quiet and consistent advocacy and action. Through repeated successful collaborations, which integrate the information literacy process into the research and writing of a paper or the research and presentation of a science fair project, for example, we teach (teachers) by example. It requires a conscious, concerted effort on the part of the library media specialist to move this concept and awareness forward.—*Audrey Church, 2007 Teaching for Learning member*

Chapter 2 This chapter, with Barbara Striplng as guide, considers another aspect of assessment. She encourages us to partner with teachers and apply instructional strategies at the most effective point for each student. This approach gives us our best measure of successful instruction, qualifying process over product. When teachers evaluate student progress, the emphasis falls on the final product. As school library media specialists, our evaluations need to focus on the progression of skill development. With library curriculum serving as the baseline for information and literacy skill instruction, our program naturally leads to focus on the expansion of those skills. Stripling's work provides us with the background we need to develop measures of student understanding, through diagnostic, formative, and summative assessments. These, in turn, provide the data we need to create collaborative partnerships in our learning community. When cooperative planning sessions begin, focused data regarding student skills can support curricular designs. Administrative requests for data-driven decisions also can be answered through the methods developed here. Comparative data, as defined in this chapter, involving various stages of student assignments, gives a clearer, more usable picture of the effectiveness of the school library program.

Assessment of Information Fluency

Author's Note: This article is based on an address delivered at the 2006 Fall Forum sponsored by the American Association of School Librarians in Providence, Rhode Island.

Teachers use a variety of assessment methods in our schools to determine how well their students have learned the content of the curriculum. Underlying that content learning is the students' abilities to use strategies and skills to make sense of the information. It is surprising, therefore, that when teachers measure content learning they do not assess how well students have learned the strategies and skills that have made that learning possible. School library media specialists (SLMSs) are in an ideal position to collaborate with teachers and develop learning skill assessments because those skills form the backbone of the library curriculum—we teach these information fluency skills in the context of content-based units.

Assessment should be integral to any inquiry-based learning experience. In the early stages of inquiry, SLMSs may want to focus on **diagnostic assessment**, moving to **formative assessment** during the active investigation phases of inquiry and to **summative assessment** at the end to determine the extent of the final learning. Figure 1 illustrates the type of assessment most effective at different stages of the inquiry process.

Barbara Stripling
Director of Library
Services, New York City
Department of Education

Diagnostic Assessment

Diagnostic assessment is the measurement of knowledge and skills before a learning experience in order to design the teaching to meet students' actual needs. It corresponds to the Connect phase of inquiry, in which students are determining their current connections to the topic and assessing their pre-existing skills. Students bring widely divergent skill sets when they come to the library for a research unit—some may have previously completed comprehensive research assignments, while others may have never even checked out a book. The SLMS can use a diagnostic assessment instrument to determine for each student what information skills are solidly in place and which ones must be taught or scaffolded.

Diagnostic assessments of information fluency do not have to be cumbersome or overly time-consuming, but they do need to offer a clear picture of the students' existing level of skills. The following techniques have proven to be successful as diagnostic tools for SLMSs:

- Ask a quick question on an entrance card completed by each student (for example, "What is Boolean logic?").
- Ask students to complete a pre-instruction task ("Find a book on _____").
- Administer a pre-test.
- Assess misconceptions by asking students to agree or disagree with statements about how to perform the skill or strategy that is being targeted.
- Ask students to complete the "K" of a K-W-L (Know-Want to Know-Learned) chart.
- Require a concept map to be filled out with pre-existing knowledge ("These are the steps I follow when I research a topic . . .").

Formative Assessment

Formative assessment is the measurement of knowledge and skills during the process of learning in order to inform the next steps of learning; it is assessment **for** learning. Information skills are taught and used during the process of learning; therefore, it makes sense to look at the attainment of skills during the inquiry process to make sure that students are successfully completing each phase before moving to the next phase. SLMSs can use formative assessment during several phases of inquiry— Wonder, Investigate, and Construct—to help them determine when to teach mini-lessons to the whole class or individuals.

Some formative assessment techniques involve observation or evaluation by the SLMS, including the following:

- Checklist of tasks that are essential for inquiry process (for example, "developed clear and researchable questions," "found at least three books," "outlined a search strategy"). The SLMS checks each student's work and ensures that each student is staying on track.
- Exit cards that students fill out before leaving the library, on which they answer a question such as "What was the most valuable resource you located today, and why?"
- Response to student learning logs, in which students keep a running record of their inquiry process, questions, struggles, and "a-ha" moments. The SLMS reads the learning logs periodically to assess student progress.
- Consultation with individual students during their inquiry process.

Other formative assessments involve student reflections on their own learning through some of the following:

- Learning logs or process logs, in which students use metacognitive skills to watch their own process of learning and identify areas of confusion or frustration.
- Responses to questions throughout the process of inquiry. These questions will help students determine if they are ready to move to the next phase of inquiry (for example, "Do I know enough about the idea or topic to ask good questions?" "Which sources will be most useful and valuable?" "Have I located sources with diverse perspectives?").
- Reciprocal teaching or sharing with another student. Students find that when they share their inquiry strategies with their peers, they often get feedback that enables them to modify their strategies and be more effective.

Probably the most effective tools of formative assessment are integral to the learning process itself—the documents created by the students in the context of the unit while they are performing a skill. These formative assessment tools are the templates, graphic organizers, and documents that students are asked to complete during the normal course of their research (for example, a note-taking template, a sheet of questions for evaluating a Web site, a graphic organizer that leads to organization by thesis and supporting points).

Summative Assessment

Summative assessment is used at the later stages of the inquiry process (Express and Reflect) to measure how well the students learned the skills taught with the unit. Much of summative assessment conducted by classroom teachers is associated with the learning of content; therefore, the SLMS may want to work with classroom teachers to integrate the assessment of process skills into the end-of-unit evaluation. Two popular forms of summative assessment are checklists and rubrics. A sample checklist for final evaluation of information fluency skills is shown in figure 2.

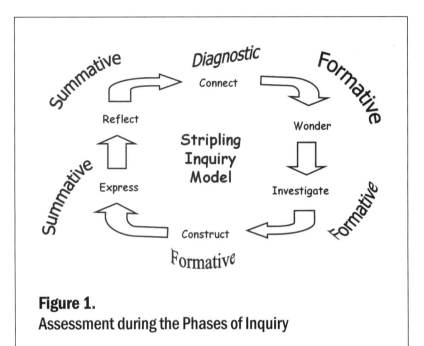

Figure 1.
Assessment during the Phases of Inquiry

	Geraldo	Chymeka	Steven	Stephanie	Jamal
Elementary:					
Predicted what a book would be about from its title					
Took notes on at least two facts to answer each question					
Used pictures to find answers to questions					
Secondary:					
Developed at least three focusing questions					
Set up note-taking log sheets with a question at the top of each					
Found and took notes from a magazine article					
Found and took notes from two books					
Evaluated a Web site using the criteria established by the class					

Figure 2.
Final Checklist of Information Fluency Skills

The measurement of pre-existing knowledge and skills and the identification of misconceptions in order to set goals for new learning	
Teacher-Led	**Learner-Led**
Pre-Test Pre-Performance Task Misconceptions Assessment	K (Know) of K-W-L Chart Concept Map

Figure 3.
Diagnostic Assessment

Statement	Agree	Disagree
1. Assessment is the same as evaluation.		
2. Authentic assessment can be defined as "alternative venues for students to demonstrate their learning."		
3. Reflection is an essential component of assessment.		
4. Assessment is out of the hands of library media specialists because information fluency skills are not tested on the standardized, NCLB-required exams.		

Figure 4.
Misconceptions Assessment

The measurement of knowledge and skills during the process of learning in order to inform the next steps	
Teacher-Led	**Learner-Led**

Ungraded Exams
Feedback on Drafts
Exit Cards
Observation Checklist
Consultation Interview
Interactive Research Journal
Progress/Benchmark Checks
Rubric
	Reflecting
	    Learning Log Note-taking
	    Progress Log
	    Process Log
	Questioning
	    Inquiry Framework Questions
	    Question Stems
	Organizing
	    Visualization
	    Concept Map
	    Simplified Outline
	Sharing
	    Reciprocal Teaching
	    Thinkaloud
	Challenging
	    Peer Review and Feedback
	    Challenging Questions: What If? Why? What Else?
	      Who Says? So What?
	Evaluating
	    Checklist
	    Rubric

Figure 5.
Formative Assessment

Guidelines for Developing Assessments of Information Fluency

Librarians can be more effective in assessing information fluency by following certain guidelines:

- establish clear information fluency learning goals;
- define clear criteria for successful application of information fluency skills;
- align goal and criteria with assignment;
- move students to self-assessment; and
- make assessments a natural part of teaching and learning.

SLMSs must accept responsibility for assessing student learning of information skills. These assessments can occur at the beginning of a process of inquiry to diagnose students' needs (diagnostic), in the middle of an inquiry assignment to form future teaching and learning experiences (formative), and at the end of an inquiry process to evaluate the final achievement of the students in learning the information skills that were taught during the unit (summative). In all cases, the assessment of students' information fluency is essential to the development of lifelong learning and information skills.

Examples of Diagnostic Assessment

Misconceptions Assessment

The teacher or SLMS begins a unit of study by giving students a list of statements and asking them to agree or disagree with them. The students do not know that some of the statements actually identify commonly held misconceptions. When the correct answers are announced, students are alerted to the misconceptions that they hold. Research has shown that unless learners recognize their own misconceptions, they are not likely to replace them with more accurate or detailed knowledge.

Concept Map

A concept map is a visualization of what a student knows about a topic, including the major ideas and the relationship among ideas. This is a useful tool at the Connect phase of inquiry, because it is important for students to recognize what they know and do not know before they start a unit of study. Concept maps also are very useful for bringing misconceptions to the surface, because students often will draw their understandings in clearer ways than they can express in words. Students can use the following process to create concept maps:

- Create a visual symbol of the main idea for the center of the map.
- Brainstorm all that you already know about the topic using visual symbols or words, writing each on a separate card or slip of paper.
- Prioritize and organize the ideas, placing the major ones in some relationship to the central idea. When you are satisfied that your organization expresses your ideas well, transfer the major ideas to the concept map. Draw appropriate connections among the ideas (arrows, straight lines, question marks).
- Add the rest of your facts and ideas to the concept map where they are most appropriately placed and show the connections and relationships among the ideas by using lines, graphics, or visual placements.

Examples of Formative Assessment

Exit Cards

The SLMS hands each student a card in the last five to ten minutes of class time in the library. Upper elementary and secondary students are given a specific question to answer about their progress or new understandings (for example, "What was the most interesting idea you learned today?" "What question(s) are you having trouble answering through your research?" "What source did you find today and how did you

	Geraldo	Chymeka	Steven	Stephanie	Jamal
Elementary:					
Predicted what a book would be about from its title					
Took notes on at least two facts to answer each question					
Used pictures to find answers to questions					
Secondary:					
Composed three or more focused questions					
Set up note-taking log sheets with a question at the top of each					
Found and took magazine notes					
Found and took notes from two books					
Evaluated a Web site using the criteria established by the class					

Figure 6.
Observation Checklist

Notes	Reactions
Learning logs can be used any time a student is responsible for writing down information (from library sources, interviews, lecture notes). Students write notes in their own words in the left column and react to those notes in the right column. The purpose of a learning log is to help students learn to interact mentally and emotionally with their notes while they are in the process of taking them. Not only do they learn more while they are taking notes, but they also can identify areas where they need additional information or different perspectives.	Reactions can include: Personal comments or feelings about the information (I think companies that dump toxic waste should be heavily fined.) Questions (What are the laws on toxic-waste dumping? What source will give me another perspective on this issue?) Notes about organization (Use this information in my introduction.) Connections to previous knowledge (Toxic-waste dumping is worse than oil spills because it's intentional. I think this information is true because it agrees with two other sources.)

Figure 7.
Learning Log Note-taking

decide it was valuable?" "Where are you in your inquiry process and what's your next step?"). Lower elementary students can be asked to rate their own progress on simplified tasks ("Did you find five facts about your animal today?") with their name and a smiley or frowny face. The students hand in the cards as they leave. The SLMS responds on the back with specific suggestions, provocative questions, ideas for next steps, or general encouragement.

The measurement of knowledge and skills at the end of a process of learning in order to determine the amount and quality of learning	
Teacher-Led	**Learner-Led**
Authentic Product	Concept Map
Presentation or Exhibition	Final Reflection
Performance Task	Authentic Product
Portfolio/ Process Folio	Presentation or Exhibition
Checklist	Portfolio/ Process Folio
Rubric	Checklist
	Rubric

Figure 8.
Summative Assessment

Characteristics of Authentic Learning	Characteristics of Authentic Assessment
Worthwhile, significant, and meaningful	An authentic assessment product allows students to demonstrate meaningful answers to important questions.
Construction of knowledge	An authentic assessment product requires students to construct meaning rather than simply copy facts. The meaning is converted to understanding when students are expected to apply their knowledge and skills in a new context through creation of their assessment product.
Disciplined inquiry	The information fluency skills embedded in a framework of inquiry provide the structure and mental discipline that lead to authentic learning and assessment.
Value beyond school	Authentic assessment has value beyond the classroom because the ideas have real-world significance, the student has discovered personal connections to them, and the product has a real context or format.

Figure 9.
Authentic Assessment

Observation Checklist

Because information fluency assessment is largely a measure of students' ability to do, SLMSs can develop checklists of observable behaviors that signify students' use of information fluency skills. Checklists measure completion of work, but generally are not a good instrument to measure quality of work. Observation checklists are most valuable when developed as a matrix with students' names on one side and the observable behaviors on the other.

Inquiry Framework Questions

Students should reflect throughout their inquiry experience in order to self-regulate their progress through this recursive process. See the questions before and after each phase of inquiry in the appendix.

Reciprocal Teaching

Students pair with a fellow student to teach a new understanding they have gained about the content or process of their inquiry. Elementary students, for example, might explain how they used the table of contents and index to find information on their topics. Secondary students might teach their peers how they figured out what were the main ideas and what was supporting evidence. Students should be given a protocol to follow:

- Student One teaches for five to ten minutes, with the other student taking brief notes.
- The other student asks clarifying questions for two to three minutes to be sure he or she understands what the first student said ("Did you say . . . ?" "What did you mean when you said . . . ?").
- The other student asks probing questions for five to ten minutes to figure out why certain decisions were made and how he or she might use the same strategies ("How did you figure out the words to use in the index?").
- The students switch roles and go through the process again.

Characteristics of Summative Assessment

Authentic Assessment

The characteristics of authentic learning identified by Fred M. Newmann et al. in *A Guide to Authentic Instruction and Assessment: Vision, Standards, and Scoring* (Madison, Wisc.: Wisconsin Center for Education Research, 1995) may be translated into characteristics of authentic assessment.

Assessment Products at Different Levels of Thinking

Summative assessment products can be designed for different levels of thinking, depending on the requirements of the assignment and the depth of learning expected. If students are offered choices in assessment products to allow for different learning styles, then the alternatives must be carefully designed so that they require the same level of thinking (for example, a Hall of Fame poster does not require the same level of thinking as a debate). SLMSs can collaborate with classroom teachers to design assessment products that challenge students to think, connect, construct, and demonstrate their learning in creative and enjoyable ways.

Verbs can be used as starters for brainstorming about summative assessment products. If the verbs categorize levels of thinking, then educators can design products that match the expectations of the assignment.

The following is an adapted excerpt from Barbara K. Stripling and Judy M. Pitts's *Brainstorms and Blueprints: Teaching Library Research As a Thinking Process* (Englewood, Colo.: Libraries Unlimited, 1988):

Level	Verbs	Sample Assessment Products
Recalling Recalling and reporting the main facts discovered; Making no attempt to analyze the information or reorganize it for comparison purposes	Arrange; cluster; define; find; identify; label; list; locate; match; name; recall; recount; repeat; reproduce; select; sort; state	**Select** five to ten accomplishments of the person you have researched. Produce a "Hall of Fame" (or "Hall of Shame") poster with your biographee's photocopied picture and list of accomplishments. **List** five "Dos and Dont's" about a social issue that you have researched. Based on your research, **state** five questions a television reporter might ask if he/she were preparing a feature news story on your subject. Answer the questions.
Analyzing Breaking a subject into its component parts (causes, effects, problems, solutions); Comparing one part with another	Analyze; apply; arrange; associate; break down; categorize; change; characterize; classify; compare; compile; construct; contrast; correlate; diagram; differentiate; discriminate; dissect; distinguish; divide; examine; group; interpret; map; modify; organize; outline; question; reconstruct; relate; rewrite; scrutinize; select; separate; sequence; sift; simplify; solve; transplant; verify	**Construct** a carefully organized Web page to examine a social issue. **Characterize** your researched historical person in an obituary, which makes clear his/her role in the conflicts of the day. **Compare** your lifestyle and neighborhood to those of people living in the time you have researched. Write a letter to the editor **scrutinizing** a local issue. Support your opinions with specific details from your research.
Transforming Bringing together more than one piece of information, forming own conclusion, and presenting that conclusion in a creative new format	Blend; build; combine; compile; compose; conclude; construct; convince; create; decide; design; develop; dramatize; elaborate; express; forecast; formulate; generate; imagine; modify; persuade; plan; predict; pretend; produce; propose; revise; speculate; structure	**Design** and **produce** a television commercial or a whole advertising campaign that presents your research results to the class. **Create** a board game that incorporates the major conclusions you reached about your researched subject. Write a poem or short story that **expresses** your new knowledge or insight. **Dramatize** a famous historical event. The dramatization should make clear your interpretation of the event. **Compose** a speech that a historical person might deliver about a present-day national issue. Compose a speech that a current public person might deliver about a historical issue.

Figure 10.
Assessment Products at Different Levels of Thinking

Guidelines for Developing Assessments of Information Fluency

- establish clear information fluency learning goals;
- define clear criteria for successful application of information fluency skills;
- align goals and criteria with assignment;
- move to student self-assessment; and
- make assessments a natural part of teaching and learning throughout the process of learning.

Appendix. New York City School Library System Information Fluency Continuum Framework and Key Indicators

STANDARD 1: USING INQUIRY TO BUILD UNDERSTANDING → "I am a thinker."
An independent learner asks authentic questions and accesses, evaluates, and uses information effectively to develop new understandings.

INQUIRY PHASE: CONNECT
At the beginning of the Connect Phase, a student may ask:
What interests me about this idea or topic?
What do I already know or think I know about this topic?
What background information would help me get an overview of my topic?

INDICATORS
Connects ideas to self; finds personal passion.
Connects ideas to previous knowledge.
Observes, experiences.
Gains background and context.
Identifies key concepts and terms.
Identifies the "big picture" or schema.

Before moving to the Wonder Phase, a student may ask:
Do I know enough about the idea or topic to ask good questions?
Am I interested enough in the idea or topic to investigate it?

INQUIRY PHASE: WONDER
At the beginning of the Wonder Phase, a student may ask:
What intriguing questions do I have about the topic or idea?
Why am I doing this research?
What do I expect to find?

INDICATORS
Develops and refines questions.
Recognizes purpose for inquiry.
Makes predictions about the kind of **information** needed to answer the questions and the **sources** that will be most likely to have that information.
Forms tentative thesis or hypothesis to guide research.

Before moving to the Investigate Phase, a student may ask:
Can my question(s) be answered through investigation?
Will my question(s) lead me to answers that will fulfill my assignment or purpose for research?

INQUIRY PHASE: INVESTIGATE

At the beginning of the Investigate Phase, a student may ask:

What are all of the sources that might be used?

Which sources will be most useful and valuable?

How do I locate these sources?

How do I find the information within each source?

How do I evaluate the information that I find?

INDICATORS

Understands the organization of a library.

Plans research and follows a timeline.

Uses successful information and technology strategies for locating **sources** of information.

Seeks information from diverse genres, formats, and points of view.

Examines sources to determine their usefulness.

Understands the organization of information within a resource.

Uses information strategies to locate **information** within a source.

Uses reading and thinking strategies to comprehend and make meaning from information and monitor own understanding.

Uses visual literacy strategies to derive meaning from information presented visually.

Evaluates information to determine value and relevance for answering questions.

Evaluates information for fact, opinion, point of view, and bias.

Identifies inaccurate and misleading information.

Selects and records appropriate information in reflective and interactive process.

Puts information into own words.

Identifies gaps in information.

Before moving to the Construct Phase, a student may ask:

Have I located sources with diverse perspectives?

Have I found enough accurate information to answer all my questions?

Have I discovered information gaps and filled them with more research?

Have I begun to identify relationships and patterns and thoughtfully reacted to the information I found?

INQUIRY PHASE: CONSTRUCT

At the beginning of the Construct Phase, a student may ask:

Have any main ideas emerged from the research?

Did I find enough evidence to form an opinion or support my thesis?

What organizational patterns or tools will help me make sense of my information?

INDICATORS

Clarifies main and supporting ideas.

Connects ideas across texts.

Uses organizational strategies to make sense of information.

Makes sense of information by using appropriate thinking strategies.

Compares new ideas to what was already known.

Tests statement of purpose and thesis statement or hypothesis.

Draws conclusions.

Before moving to the Express Phase, a student may ask:

Have I drawn conclusions that are supported by the evidence?

Have I organized my conclusions and evidence to present them effectively?

INQUIRY PHASE: EXPRESS

At the beginning of the Express Phase, a student may ask:

What type of product or presentation will allow me to present my conclusions and evidence effectively to the intended audience?

What technology will help me create a product or presentation?

How will I get help to revise and edit my product?

INDICATORS

Uses writing process to develop expression of new understandings.

Creates products and communicates results in a variety of formats.

Uses standard language and citation conventions.

Uses technology tools to create products.

Develops strategies for revision.

Develops creative products to express ideas and information.

Before moving to the Reflect Phase, a student may ask:

Have I organized the product/presentation to make my major points and present convincing evidence?

Does my product/presentation fulfill all the requirements of the assignment?

INQUIRY PHASE: REFLECT

At the beginning of the Reflect Phase, a student may ask:

Is my product/presentation as effective as I can make it?

How well did my inquiry process go?

How can I get feedback on my final product to use in my next inquiry project?

INDICATORS

Develops evaluative criteria.

Participates in peer evaluation.

Engages in self-evaluation.

Asks new questions for continuing inquiry.

Before moving to another assignment or personal inquiry, a student may ask:

What new understandings did I develop about the topic or idea?

What did I learn about inquiry?

What new questions do I now want to answer about the topic or idea?

STANDARD 2: PURSUING PERSONAL AND AESTHETIC GROWTH → "I am an explorer."

An independent learner responds to and creates literary and artistic expressions, uses effective strategies for personal exploration of ideas, and reads on his or her own by choice.

LITERARY/ARTISTIC RESPONSE AND EXPRESSION

INDICATORS

Connects to and forms personal meaning from literary and artistic works.

Deepens understanding of literature by analyzing the parts.

Selects appropriate texts from a variety of genres.

Understands author's purpose and voice.

Makes connections across works of literature or art.

Discusses, evaluates, and shares great literature.

Creates personal responses to literature using arts and technology.

PERSONAL EXPLORATION

INDICATORS

Uses technology to solve real-world problems.

Locates reliable information for personal growth.

Uses technology for personal and career growth.

Uses arts and technology for personal expression.

MOTIVATED, INDEPENDENT LEARNING

INDICATORS

Locates and selects materials of interest in a variety of genres.

Uses text features to increase understanding.

Reads for a variety of purposes.

Uses multiple ways to access resources.

Seeks to understand the meaning of what is read.

Seeks information related to personal interests.

Uses technology to find information related to personal interests.

STANDARD 3: DEMONSTRATING SOCIAL RESPONSIBILITY → "I am a citizen."

An independent learner contributes to the learning community by seeking multiple perspectives, sharing his or her understandings with others, and using information and resources ethically.

IMPORTANCE OF INFORMATION TO A DEMOCRATIC SOCIETY

INDICATORS

Seeks diverse sources and multiple points of view.

Respects the principle of equitable access to information.

Understands that democracy is built on access to information without censorship.

EFFECTIVE SOCIAL INTERACTION TO BROADEN UNDERSTANDING

INDICATORS

Shares knowledge and information with others.

Respects others' ideas and backgrounds, and acknowledges their contributions.

Collaborates with others to solve problems.

Collaborates with others to access and use information effectively.

Uses technology to collaborate with others.

Uses a variety of media to share information with others.

ETHICAL BEHAVIOR IN USE OF INFORMATION

INDICATORS

Respects the principles of intellectual freedom.

Respects intellectual property rights.

Uses information technology responsibly.

Chapter 3 The school library media specialist (SLMS) requires new skills in a testing environment. Recognition of trends and the ability to interpret scores are part of the tools Judith Dzikowski sharpens in this chapter. Identifying question relevance, denoting subjectivity, locating curricular links, and developing an action plan are important pieces of the knowledgeable SLMS toolbox. Partnering with faculty in studying the results of recent tests provides a golden opportunity to use these tools for guiding curriculum development. Identifying which areas need to be addressed and helping to form the instructional plan ensures a united effort of the entire faculty. Dzikowski's explanations and examples highlight the various components of the testing process. Armed with this understanding, the discerning SLMS can now participate in the evaluation and curriculum development processes.

Item Analysis

What Skills Are Needed to Answer Standardized Assessment Questions? What Is the Connection to the School Library Media Program?

Author's Note: This article is based on breakout sessions (elementary, middle, and high school) delivered at the 2006 Fall Forum sponsored by the American Association of School Librarians in Warwick, Rhode Island.

In 2005–2006, the Onondaga-Cortland-Madison Counties Board of Cooperative Educational Services (OCM BOCES) School Library System and School Quality Services collaborated to design the pilot program Partners in Achievement: Libraries and Students (PALS) Improving Student Achievement through Data Use for Library Media Specialists to address the challenge of improving library instruction in information literacy skills and strategies and in library collections, by linking to identified student learning needs based on English language arts (ELA) assessment data. Guidelines and strategies for analyzing student work and skills required for collaborative dialogue were developed. The resulting identification of student learning needs was applied to collection development, library instruction, and lesson design done in collaboration with classroom teacher instruction in information literacy skills.

Training addressed the key areas of the New York State (NYS) ELA assessments, data analysis and collection development. The assessment training addressed the nature and format of the NYS ELA grades four through eight assessments. Topics included question analysis and consideration of the information literacy skills identified, the ELA 3–8 Core Curriculum, and grades three through eight standardized tests. Using data analysis tools, we focused on analyzing assessment results, identifying performance and trends gaps, and establishing the connection between NYS standards, the AASL Information Literacy Standards, and test questions. The collection development component included examination of

Judith Dzikowski
Director, School Library System, Onondaga-Cortland-Madison BOCES, Syracuse, New York

Contributor, Mary Tiedemann
Teacher-Librarian, School Library System, Onondaga-Cortland-Madison BOCES, Syracuse, New York

the school curriculum and various collection analysis reports that guided the selection of targeted materials in various formats. With this combined knowledge, teacher-librarians were able to strengthen their instructional practices.

Receiving the AASL 2006 Highsmith Research Grant Award allowed eleven teacher-librarians the opportunity for summer professional development in the PALS project to create a customized two-year library program action plan based on the information gathered through analysis of their test data, collection needs, district initiatives, and student learning needs.

A component of the PALS project was to analyze specific items on the assessments to determine the skills required for student success and to connect the identified skills to information literacy skills instruction.

Item analysis is defined as examining individual items on standardized tests that students are required to answer.

There are two types of item analysis—analysis of test questions (multiple choice, constructed response, document-based questions, essays, and listening) and analysis of group student performance (standardized and teacher-created test scores). Analyzing test questions enables us to understand the demands of the standardized tests

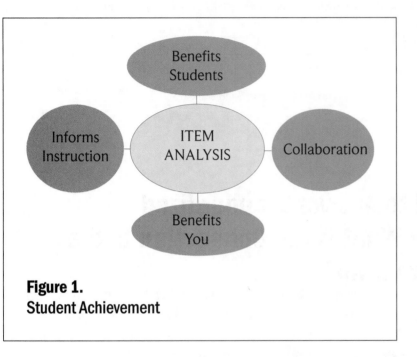

Figure 1.
Student Achievement

and develop language that is consistent with the test questions and the language the classroom teachers use. Additional considerations for item analysis are: analyze errors, content coverage, and trend analysis.

The components of item analysis include format, skills, content, and connections:

- Format—What do the questions look like? Let us look at the language used (main idea, most likely, probably, characterized by); physical arrangement (top to bottom, side by side); and the use of charts, pictures, graphic organizers, and multistep questions.
- Skills—What do students need to be able to do? Skill examples include drawing conclusions; fact versus opinion; decoding; determining meaning of words based on related content; use of various tools, including calculator, ruler, and so on; and interpretation of charts, tables, and graphs.
- Content—What do students need to know and understand? Content examples include the need for prior knowledge, the need to refer to the related passage, and vocabulary related to the specific content area.
- What connections can be made between the state standards (in NYS ELA, Information and Understanding, Literary Response and Expression, Critical Analysis and Evaluation, and Social Interaction) and the AASL Information Literacy Standards? We focused on the three standards in Category 1—Information Literacy, which are Standard 1—Accesses information efficiently and effectively; Standard 2—Evaluates information critically and competently; and Standard 3—Uses information effectively and creatively.

The AASL standards and skills are integral to all content areas. Mastery of these standards and skills provides students with a foundation for success in these and all subject areas. It is the teacher-librarian's role to identify the relationship to the information literacy skills, partnering with the classroom teacher to support district initiatives and bring to the forefront the school library media program's contribution to improving student achievement.

To begin making the connections, we need to identify the subskills that have been tested. For example, in ELA Grade 8 they are *compare and contrast information,* understand stated information, use text to understand vocabulary, and draw conclusions and make inferences. How do these subskills correlate to the AASL Information Literacy Standards? For example, in the subskill compare and contrast information, the correlations to the AASL Standards are: Standard 1—Indicator 4, identifies a variety of potential sources of information; Standard 2—Indicator 1, determines accuracy, relevance, and comprehensiveness; and Standard 3—Indicator 1, organizes information for practical application. In the subskill *draw conclusions and make inferences,* the AASL Standard 3—Indicator 3, integrates new information in critical thinking and problem solving.

In review, the key concepts to consider include

- Standardized tests are not recall of facts.
- Students are required to use critical-thinking skills.
- There are connections between the state standards and the AASL Standards.
- Teacher-librarians are partners with classroom teachers on instruction.
- Mastery of the AASL Standards is critical for student success in all subject areas.
- Knowledge of the connections helps to inform our instruction.

Analysis of student performance is the examination of scores on standardized and teacher-created tests. Standardized tests compare the performance of a group of students in an area to the performance of a larger sample group in order to identify performance gaps or strengths. They do not measure individual student success. It is a snapshot of one day and one measurement tool.

Warning!!! In general, state-level assessments are NOT designed to be diagnostic of individual student performance. There are other tools that are better at individual diagnostics. A diagnostic assessment is designed differently than a summative assessment that is used for the purpose of accountability. So the obvious question is, "So why do we want to do this work?" With an understanding of the test it is possible to use the data for program analysis, that is, to look at the effectiveness of our educational programs for groups of students.

What does *analyzing student performance* accomplish? You will be able to

- identify where students are successful;
- identify gaps in content areas;
- identify specific skills and trends over years; and
- highlight points of reference for collaboration.

Remember: A low percentage of right answers does not necessarily indicate a problem; it could be a question aimed at the top-level students, which is why comparing data with other similar schools is important.

This analysis provides compelling data that can be used to inform instruction. In addition, it must be recognized that reflection on the results of teacher-created measurements of student achievement is a vital component of comprehensive assessment and analysis.

In conclusion, item analysis is a powerful tool that can empower the teacher-librarian by providing information that will inform instruction and collaboration with classroom teachers on lesson unit development focused on targeted gaps in student performance as measured on standardized tests. Teacher-librarians are collaborators with a global perspective on students that is unique and highly valuable, benefiting the students by enabling them to access, evaluate, use, synthesize, and interpret information that will lead them to success!

Chapter 4 Now that the when and where of the assessment puzzle have been considered, Marjorie Pappas gathers various methods of how. Although measurement may sometimes be considered as part of our final analysis, we can always use additional methods for ongoing instructional planning purposes. This chapter pulls together a valuable compilation of various modes of information collection and organization. Directives for student analysis, methodical organizers, and self-help journaling are a few of the tools offered to aid all of us in expanding student cognition. Your own progress through this portion will help to gather measurable data through evaluations of individual and group projects. These pieces will help in the collection of data to support discussions in collaborative efforts for schoolwide responses to test assessments.

The Tools of Assessment

Author's Note: This article is based on a keynote address delivered at the 2006 Fall Forum sponsored by the American Association of School Librarians in Providence, Rhode Island.

Standards-based education and No Child Left Behind require educators to be accountable for documenting learner achievement. Classroom teachers are focused on gathering evidence to show that learners meet or exceed the content area standards, especially in reading, language arts, and math. Much of that evidence is gathered through the state tests based on standards that have been established by educators within each state.

The curriculum of the school library media program is based on the *Information Literacy Standards for Student Learning* (AECT and AASL 1998). Many states include school library media or information literacy standards integrated throughout the state standards or in a separate standards document. For example, the North Carolina Standard Course of Study includes Information Skills, one of the content areas curriculums. The Indiana Standards include information skills throughout the document. In addition, school library media specialists (SLMSs) identified benchmarks in every curricular area that correlate with the *Information Literacy Standards for Student Learning*. When teachers and SLMSs use the *Indiana Academic Standards* (2007), the correlation between the content area standards and information literacy is clearly presented and facilitates collaboration between classroom teachers and SLMSs. Harada suggests that information literacy skills can be found within most state standards, but the connections between these and school library media programs are not clearly evident. SLMSs need to become actively engaged in creating documents that show this connection. Indiana SLMSs have developed a model for a collaborative effort that other states should follow.

Marjorie L. Pappas
Virtual Professor, Writer, and Consultant, Rutgers University, Danville, Kentucky

Inquiry Learning and Assessment

Information Power includes a significant focus on constructivist learning theory, which is the foundation for inquiry learning. "Inquiry requires students to be active rather than passive learners" and to engage in questioning, thinking, making connections between ideas, and constructing new knowledge (Pappas and Tepe 2002, 27). Stripling and Hughes-Hassell (2003, 6) suggest that inquiry "is a relationship between thinking skills and content." In a constructivist learning environment, assessment is focused on student work as evidence of students' ability to apply information literacy skills and engage in inquiry. Harada (2006) believes assessment is the "process of collecting, analyzing and reporting data that informs us about progress and problems a learner encounters in a learning experience." Assessment occurs throughout the learning experience and can range from observing to reflecting in learning logs or journals to thinking as documented through organizers, checklists, rating scales, and rubrics.

When SLMSs begin to use assessment tools, some basic understandings include:

- Tools facilitate both learning and assessment.
- The use of tools is developmental, and students will need experience using tools.
- Student use of learning and assessment tools independently is the ultimate goal.

Logs, Journals, and Reflection

Logs and journals engage students in thinking about their process and the learning experience. Writing prompts are important for focusing students on the goals or objectives. Logs encourage students to think about what they learned, how they learned, and how they feel about the experience. For example, writing prompts for elementary students might include:

- The three most important things I learned today are _____.
- Resources I used to find information include _____.
- Today my learning experience was enjoyable/not enjoyable because _____.

In another example, the learning goal engaged students in finding information from a subscription database. Writing prompts could include:

- Some new and relevant information I located about my research question includes _____.
- My most successful search strategies include _____.
- Words that describe my feelings when I used the database include _____.

Checklists

A checklist is a list of the requirements for a project or assignment. Checklists help students understand the steps and required elements of a project and can help students reflect on the status of the project through-out the time they are working. The checklist can help the teacher or SLMS monitor the student's progress, provide feedback during the assignment, and facilitate the final assessment of the project. Some information that checklists provide include:

- identifies behaviors;
- focuses on critical aspects of the task; and
- provides evidence of learning and new knowledge.

Figure 1 shows an example checklist.

Rubrics

Information Power (AECT and AASL 1998, 177) defines a rubric as "a scaled set of criteria that clearly defines for the student and the teacher what a range of acceptable and unacceptable performances looks like." Teachers sometimes provide examples of a project or an assignment along with the rubric to give students both the specific performance criteria at different levels and an illustration of the completed project. Ideally, a rubric should be developed with students so they have a role in establishing the performance criteria. An effective rubric can be used by students as a learning tool and by teachers as a tool to assess performance. Rubrics should include the following components:

	Yes	No
I can use the catalog to find information on my topic.		
I can use the Dewey number to find books on the shelf.		
I can use an index to find information in my book.		
I can write a citation for my book.		

Figure 1.
Checklist Example

- components of the task;
- criteria for quality product; and
- ranges of performance.

Effective rubrics can be a challenge to write. Tool Web sites such as RubiStar <http://rubistar.4teachers. org/index.php> are good places to begin developing rubrics. Sometimes it is helpful to use a checklist or rating scale the first time students complete an assignment. Those documents will be helpful in developing the criteria and performance descriptors of the rubric for the next time the assignment is used with students. Also, select several of the best assignments to use as examples in the future. Always ask students for permission to use their work in this manner—those documents are their intellectual property.

Organizers

Organizers are tools that enable students to visualize relationships and make connections (Pappas and Tepe 2002). Harada and Yoshina (2005, 49) suggest "graphic organizers are visual representations of thinking." Organizers include concept maps, matrices, and K-W-L charts. Webs and mind maps are another organizer tool. Hyerle (1996, 36) suggests,

Brainstorming webs "are used to develop students' fluency with thinking. . . . Fluency is the capacity to flow flexibly from idea to idea within and across disciplines, easily make interconnections among ideas, sustain inquiry over time, openly pursue alternative points of view, question and possibly discard hardened opinions."

Organizers are used as learning tools in many disciplines. For example:

The math discipline uses Venn diagrams to examine numerical relationships. Flow charts are used to illustrate a decision-making process in math and computer science. The language arts teachers have been using webs to explore relationships of characters and plot in fiction stories (Pappas 1997, 30).

There are different types of organizers, but the most common are listed below:

- concept maps
  visual diagrams to show links among important related concepts
- webs
  graphic organizers that cluster words around a central topic or theme
- matrices
  grids to show similarities and differences
- K-W-L charts
  charts for planning and assessing projects

Many examples of organizers within these categories can be found on the Web and in books focused on inquiry, information literacy skills, and content area lessons. A selection of both books and Web sites can be found in the Tools Pathfinder (Pappas). Also, school library periodicals often include sample information skills lessons with organizers and other assessment tools.

Thinking Skills and Organizers

Organizers enable students to visually represent their thinking. The example in figure 2 demonstrates the thinking skill of comprehension.

Application of critical-thinking skills can be found in many state standards and benchmarks across all content areas. Bloom's Taxonomy provides a hierarchy of thinking skills, which are often used as a framework for writing standards and objectives. How are thinking skills reflected within information literacy? Harada's (2003, 44–45) perception of thinking processes includes:

- storage and retrieval of data;
- organization and transformation of data; and
- reasoning and use of information.

As students apply these thinking processes, critical thinking is evident, and connections between various content areas and information literacy skills provide opportunities for collaboration between classroom teachers and SLMSs. Organizers are an appropriate tool for both the learning and assessment of these thinking processes. Some examples are shown in figure 3.

Each of the organizers in these examples provides students with a learning tool to engage in the thinking process. The completed organizer also demonstrates the students' ability to effectively apply the thinking process.

Organizers and Process

Many SLMSs engage students in using a process model as they gather, evaluate, and use information. Callison and Lamb (2006) place process models into the following categories:

- information search and use models;
- models that apply information literacy to inquiry;
- information inquiry models; and
- composition models.

Information Inquiry models include the Inquiry Cycle (Loertscher and Woolls), 8-Ws Model (Lamb), and the Research Cycle (McKenzie). Models that apply Information Literacy to Inquiry include the NYC Inquiry Fluency Model (Stripling and Hughes-Hassell 2003) and Pathways to Knowledge (Pappas and Tepe 2002). Each of these models includes steps that are typically represented within content area standards. For example, the 8-Ws Model includes the following:

Weaving. (Synthesizing) consists of organizing ideas, creating models, and formulating plans. It focuses on the application, analysis, and synthesis of information (Callison and Lamb 2006).

	Ponds	Forests	Oceans
Birds	Geese	Hawks	Sea gulls
Mammals	Beavers	Bears	Whales
Reptiles	Painted turtles	Rubber boas	Sea turtles

Figure 2.
Comprehension Thinking Skill Example

Thinking Process	Information Literacy Strategy	Organizers
Storage and retrieval of data	Evaluate resources based on relevance	Use a matrix to compare resources for relevancy to the research question
Organization and transformation of data	Organize information based on a sequence of events	Develop a timeline that demonstrates the sequence of historical events
Reasoning and use of information	Analyze information to develop a conclusion for a research project	Use a three-circle Venn diagram

Figure 3.
Organizer Examples

The *Indiana Academic Standards* (2007) in social studies (eighth grade) includes this standard:

Form historical research questions and seek responses by analyzing primary resources—such as autobiographies, diaries, maps, photographs, letters, and government documents—and secondary resources, such as biographies and other nonfiction books and articles on the history of the United States.

An Indiana SLMS who has been teaching eighth-grade students to use the 8-Ws Model might review with beginning steps of Wandering (Questioning), Webbing (Searching), and Wiggling (Evaluating) but concentrate the lesson focus on the Weaving step. Part of the lesson plan could include using a matrix organizer to facilitate analysis of a selection of primary source documents. When students have completed their matrix organizer, both the classroom teacher and the SLMS can examine the analysis matrices that demonstrate students' thinking processes related to analysis and their ability to apply the Weaving (Synthesizing) step of the 8-Ws process model.

An example of an "Artifact Analysis Matrix" on *The Learning Page* includes the following questions:

- What objectives observations do you have about the artifact?
- What questions might you ask?
- What inferences might you make to answer the questions?

Inquiry Process Steps	Related Organizers
Finding a focus	Webs, K-W-L charts
Planning for inquiry	Planning matrix
Collect and evaluate information	T-Chart for recording information, matrix to evaluate information
Organize and present new knowledge	Sequence, analyze, synthesize, and evaluate

Figure 4.
Organizer Examples

Process	Strategies	Planned Date to Finish	Actual Completion Date
My focus	Brainstorm topic with webbing (Inspiration) Use KWL to develop questions		
My research question(s)	Develop research question(s) from questions on the KWL chart		
My search strategies	Develop keywords from Brainstorm list of tools (e.g., catalog, databases, search engines, subject directories) and resources (e.g., books, Web sites, periodical articles from full text databases, etc.) Use search strategy organizer		
Recording information	Use T-Chart organizer		
Creating my product	Decide on format Use Inspiration to organize information Delegate parts of project to group members		
Evaluate my process and product	Use checklist (or rubric), complete personal reflection		

Figure 5.
Plan Development Example

Student responses to these and other questions on the matrix for several artifacts would demonstrate students' ability to analyze artifacts and to apply the Weaving step of the process model.

A generic series of steps for an inquiry process appears in the left column of figure 4 with a collection of organizers that might be applied as both learning and assessment tools.

Developing a plan is one step of an inquiry process that many students find challenging. Figure 5 shows the beginning steps of a plan. The date to finish column is important because it encourages students to develop a schedule. The date of completion column shows the students and the teacher or SLMS the actual date of completion. Often students wait until the night before to work on their project, and the outcome demonstrates that lack of planning. Planning is an important skill and should be included in the assessment.

Recording information is one of the most challenging steps in the inquiry process. One very useful organizer for this step is a T-Chart. The left column can include concise summaries of the content from a resource and perhaps a few very short quotations (always with quotation marks). The second column can be used for analysis and evaluation of the information. Some writing prompts can be helpful as part of this column to facilitate both analysis and evaluation. A section of the form might include prompts for citation elements. Teachers or the SLMS can create this form and have it available in the classroom or library media center for student use. Also, a digital copy of the form might be stored on the library media center's Web site for students who want to record information on their computers. Figure 6 is an example of a T-Chart.

Using Assessment Information

Assessment tools document questions, process, and thinking, while evaluation, the traditional testing approach, "evaluates students' ability to regurgitate information" (Pappas 2007). Testing provides educators, parents, and lawmakers with statistical data based on test results. The documentation from assessment is more challenging to quantify. How might learning be designed with a focus on assessment? Koechlin and Zwaan (2003) suggest the following strategies:

- ask what students should know or be able to do;
- ask what tools will provide evidence of new knowledge or skills;
- develop the learning experiences;
- design the tools to collect evidence;
- reflect on and analyze that evidence; and
- share and use new information to design future learning experiences.

Citation: Author: Title: Publisher:		Place: Date:
Content Notes	**My Reaction**
Write a summary (one paragraph) that includes the major ideas from this resource.	How do I know my information is accurate? Current? Free of bias?
What are one or two short quotations I might find useful?	How do other sources support this perspective?
	How does this information provide a response to my research question?

Figure 6.
T-Chart Example

Build Your Own Information Literate School by Koechlin and Zwaan (2003) includes a collection of lessons focused on information literacy skills. Each skill lesson is written on the Novice, Apprentice, and InfoStar levels, and SLMSs would find these helpful as they collaborate with teachers and teach information literacy skills. The final chapter of this book focuses on designing and using assessment to improve instruction and to document students' ability to apply information skills in an aggregate format. This form of assessment will not provide SLMSs with statistical data equivalent to the data provided by the state tests. However, SLMSs who have analyzed the state standards for those standards that correlate with the Information Literacy Standards for Student Learning have a means of documenting students' ability to apply information literacy skills relative to content area standards, which ultimately will demonstrate the relationship between the school library media program and the curriculum of the school. Although anecdotal rather than quantitative, over time that evidence can be very useful.

For example, state standards typically include the standard "Students can gather and evaluate information." SLMSs who systematically gather assessment documentation using reflection logs, rubrics, checklists, and organizers and record that data by classes will develop a profile reflecting the information skills of each grade level and the correlation with the content curriculum. That evidence might be shared with school administrators, teachers, and parents periodically to demonstrate the contributions of the library media program.

Should SLMSs try to collect this information every time they teach an information literacy lesson? Given the student-to-SLMS ratio, that would be impossible. However, SLMSs might select lessons or collaborative projects shared with classroom teachers periodically that cover the scope of the information literacy or library media curriculum and collect and retain information from those assessments. A selective but systematic collection will result in useful assessment information, and comparisons across several years might demonstrate the information skill and inquiry capability of those classes who regularly take advantage of the library media program.

Works Cited

ALTEC, University of Kansas. 2006. RubiStar. <http://rubistar.4teachers.org/index.php> (accessed 7 Mar. 2007).

Association for Educational Communications and Technology and American Association of School Librarians (AECT and AASL). 1998. *Information Power: Building Partnerships for Learning.* Chicago: ALA.

Callison, Danny, and Annette Lamb. 2006. Information Age Inquiry. <http://virtualinquiry.com/inquiry/ws.htm> (accessed 7 Mar. 2007).

Harada, Violet H. 2003. "Empowered Learning: Fostering Thinking Across the Curriculum." In *Curriculum Connections through the Library.* Ed. Barbara K. Stripling and Sandra Hughes-Hassell. Westport, Conn.: Libraries Unlimited.

Harada, Violet H. 2006. "What is Assessment?" AASL Fall Forum. Warwick, R.I., October 2006.

Harada, Violet H., and Joan M. Yoshina. 2005. *Assessing Learning: Librarians and Teachers As Partners.* Westport, Conn.: Libraries Unlimited.

Hyerle, David. 1996. *Visual Tools for Constructing Knowledge.* Alexandria, Va.: ASCD.

Indiana Department of Education. 2007. *Indiana's Academic Standards.* <http://www.doe.state.in.us/standards/ILS_Correlations.html> (accessed 7 Mar. 2007).

Information Age Inquiry. 2005. <http://virtualinquiry.com/inquiry/index.htm> (accessed 7 Mar. 2007).

Koechlin, Carol, and Sandi Zwaan. 2003. *Build Your Own Information Literate School.* Salt Lake City: Hi Willow.

Library of Congress. 2002. "Artifact Analysis Matrix." The Learning Page. <http://memory.loc.gov/learn/lessons/99/road/matrix.html> (accessed 7 Mar. 2007).

Public Schools of North Carolina. n.d. Information Skills: North Carolina Standard Course of Study. <http://www.ncpublicschools.org/curriculum/information> (accessed 7 Mar. 2007).

Pappas, Marjorie. 1997. "Organizing Research." *School Library Media Activities Monthly* 14, no. 4: 30–32.

Pappas, Marjorie L. 2006. "Tools of Assessment." AASL Fall Forum. Warwick, R.I., October 2006.

Pappas, Marjorie L., and Ann E. Tepe. 2002. *Pathways to Knowledge and Inquiry Learning.* Greenwood Village, Colo.: Libraries Unlimited.

Stripling, Barbara K., and Sandra Hughes-Hassell, eds. 2003. *Curriculum Connections through the Library.* Westport, Conn.: Libraries Unlimited.

U.S. Department of Education. n.d. No Child Left Behind. <http://www.ed.gov/nclb/landing.jhtml> (accessed 7 Mar. 2007).

Assessment Tools Pathfinder

Scope

Assessment tools include logs, checklists, rating scales, rubrics, organizers, and webs.

Keywords

Brainstorming, concept mapping, K-W-L charts, webs, graphic organizers

Books

Ausubel, David. *Learning Theory and Classroom Practice*. Ontario: The Ontario Institute for Studies in Education, 1967.

The Critical Thinking Co. Organizing Thinking Books 1 and 2: Organizers on CD. <http://www.criticalthinking.com/getProductDetails.do?code=c&id=06808>.

Harada, Violet H., and Joan M. Yoshina. *Assessing Learning*. Westport, Conn.: Libraries Unlimited.

Harada, Violet H., and Joan M. Yoshina. *Inquiry Learning through Librarian-Teacher Partnerships.*

Worthington, Ohio: Linworth, 2004.

Hyerle, David. *A Field Guide to Using Visual Tools*. ASCD, 2000.

Hyerle, David. *Visual Tools for Constructing Knowledge*. ASCD, 1996.

Kagan Cooperative Learning. Smart Cards. <http://www.kaganonline.com/Catalog/SmartCards1.html>.

Koechlin, Carol, and Sandi Zwaan. *Build Your Own Information Literate School*. Salt Lake City: Hi Willow, 2003.

Parks, Sandra, and Howard Black. *Organizing Thinking: Book 1 and 2*. Seaside, Calif.: Critical Thinking Books and Software, 1992.

Articles

Callison, Daniel. "Organizers." *School Library Media Activities Monthly* 16, no. 5 (2000): 36–39.

Harada, Violet H. "Working Smarter: Being Strategic about Assessment and Accountability." *Teacher Librarian* 33, no. 1 (Oct. 2005): 8–15.

Harada, Violet H. "Building Evidence Folders for Learning through Library Media Centers." *School Library Media Activities Monthly* 23, no. 3 (Nov. 2006): 25–29.

Harada, Violet H. and Joan M. Yoshina. "Assessing Learning: The Missing Piece in Instruction." *School Library Media Activities Monthly* 23, no. 3 (Nov. 2006): 25–29.

Pappas, Marjorie L. "Organizing Research." *School Library Media Activities Monthly* 14, no. 4 (1997): 30–32.

Pappas, Marjorie L. "State Landmarks." *School Library Media Activities Monthly* 19, no. 9 (May 2003): 22–25.

Pappas, Marjorie L. "Writing Editorials." *School Library Media Activities Monthly* 19, no. 10 (June 2003): 20–24.

Pearson Education, Inc. "Assessment: The Advantages of Rubrics." *Teacher Vision*. <http://www.teachervision.fen.com/teaching-methods/rubrics/4522.html?detoured=1> (accessed 28 Sept. 2006).

Repman, Judi. "Information Literacy and Assessment: Web Resources Too Good to Miss." *Library Talk* 15, no. 2 (Mar./Apr. 2002): 12–13.

Yoshina, Joan, and Violet H. Harada. "The Missing Link: One Elementary School's Journey with Assessment." *School Library Media Activities Monthly* 14, no. 7 (Mar. 1998).

Web Sites—Organizers

Houghton Mifflin. Graphic Organizers (2000). <http://www.eduplace.com/kids/hme/k_5/graphorg> (accessed 8 Sept. 2006).

Lamb, Annette, ed. "Graphic Organizers." Teacher Tap (2003). <http://eduscapes.com/tap/topic73.htm> (accessed 8 Sept. 2006).

North Central Regional Laboratory. Graphic Organizers (1988). <http://www.ncrel.org/sdrs/areas/issues/students/learning/lr1grorg.htm> (accessed 8 Sept. 2006).

Region 15 Graphic Organizers. <http://www.region15.org/curriculum/graphicorg.html> (accessed 8 Sept. 2006).

Schools of California Online Resources for Educators (S.C.O.R.E.). Graphic Organizers: Activity Bank. <http://www.sdcoe.k12.ca.us/score/actbank/torganiz.htm> (accessed 7 Sept. 2006).

The Virtual Institute. "Concept Mapping and Inspiration." <http://www.ettc.net/techfellow/inspir.htm> (accessed 8 Sept. 2006).

Write Design Online: Graphic Organizers. <http://www.writedesignonline.com/organizers> (accessed 8 Sept. 2006).

Web Sites—Rubrics and Rating Scales

ALTEC, The University of Kansas. "RubiStar: Create Rubrics for Your Project-Based Learning Activities." (2006). <http://rubistar.4teachers.org/index.php> (accessed 28 Sept. 2006).

The Educators' Network. "Rubrics for Teachers" (2000–2006). <http://www.rubrics4teachers.com> (accessed 28 Sept. 2006).

Schools of California Online Resources for Educators (S.C.O.R.E.). Rubrics: Activity Bank. <http://www.sdcoe.k12.ca.us/score/actbank/trubrics.htm> (accessed 28 Sept. 2006).

Valenza, Joyce Kasman. "Rubrics." Springfield Township High School Virtual Library. <http://mciu.org/%7Espjvweb/rubrics.html> (accessed 28 Sept. 2006).

Voices of the Participants: Assessment—How?

During the Fall Forum, audience members were asked to submit questions for evaluations and inclusion in a continuing discussion via a newly developed ALA online community. Included here are some of the most significant questions posed by the Rhode Island National Institute participants with answers generated by the Teaching for Learning Committee.

When starting from scratch, what steps should we, as media specialists, take in approaching classroom teachers to help them see the advantage of assessment through the library media center?

This question is similar to the "How do we help or nudge?" question. SLMSs would choose to identify a few classroom teachers with whom to begin the process. SLMSs would choose lessons that fit the standards or objectives of library media lessons that fit the grade level and show the compatibility, support, and benefits provided by the library lesson combined with the classroom standard.—*Robbie Nickel, Teaching for Learning, Team II member*

What educational journals would be beneficial to SMLSs to read to begin or continue to discuss SMLS issues in the language that teachers, principals, and administrators can understand?

Reading Teachers, Educational Leadership, and *Phi Delta Kappa* are a few of the recommended readings suggested.—*Marjorie Pappas*

    The NTCE publication *Language Arts* also is appropriate.—*Robbie Nickel, Teaching for Learning, Team II member*

At the elementary level with little or no collaboration in a building, what best functions would you recommend for assessment?

Aligning the library curriculum or standards with the grade-level standards is the way to show support by providing another avenue of assessment for the classroom teacher.—*Robbie Nickel, Teaching for Learning, Team II member*

Please understand that you may include assessment measures for your own instructional units. Successful correlations could begin as a comparison of class progressions through literacy skills as they are used within research units. The Zmuda handouts included in this booklet may help give you a framework to develop those correlations.—*Anita L. Vance, 2007 Teaching for Learning chair*)

If classes have very limited time for in–media center work, what are the best assessment tools to use to assess Information Fluency Skills? (Share topics/assignments were all long-term; I'm referring to short-term "projects.")

Checklists would work here for assessment. Information fluency skills could be broken down into short skills that could be taught a limited amount of time. These could then be assessed with a checklist or teacher observation.—*Robbie Nickel, Teaching for Learning, Team II member*

Examples could include finds books by author, student locates books by topic, student uses OPAC by title or author, student locates appropriate resource—these skill applications are compatible with the Pennsylvania Academic Standards for Reading, Writing, Speaking, and Listening 1.1, 1.1a, students identify and establish the purpose for reading. . . . Additionally, these same skills (locating appropriate materials and using Information Literacy research strategies) may be matched with the Reading, Writing, Speaking, and Listening Standards 1.8 Research a and b. The Pennsylvania Department of Education offers a workbook <http://www.statelibrary.state.pa.us/libraries/lib/libraries/Tool_Kit_Rev.pdf> with charts for the major learning standard correlations to *Information Power*'s Information Literacy Skill guidelines.—*Anita L. Vance, 2007 Teaching for Learning chair*

What practical activities can we do to collect evidence of the library's impact on student learning?

Student writing samples and student research portfolios could be sampled and added to our professional portfolio.—*Robbie Nickel, Teaching for Learning, Team II member*

A pre- and post-writing sample, such as presented by Vi Harada's student journal, could be most effective. Reviewing the information skill elements addressed during class instruction and the implementation involved in research projects prior to each scheduled visit would help to focus on strategies that are most productive for each class. A simple self-evaluation checklist shared by both subject and library skills teachers could become an accepted pattern for class visits. Such a tool may be patterned after *Lessons from* Library Power's *Library Surveys*—"Did you find what you needed?" "Was the online card catalog helpful?" "Were additional resources available?" "Did SLMS instructions help with locating materials?" Listings would fall on a scale of 1 to 5. . . . Space for comments allows student feedback and allows us to adjust our lessons.—*Anita L. Vance, 2007 Teaching for Learning chair*

Ross Todd provides excellent ideas and activities in his report on the Ohio study. Information is available from *Student Learning through Ohio School Libraries: The Ohio Research Study* <http://www.oelma.org/studentlearning>.—*Audrey Church, 2007 Teaching for Learning member*

Chapter 5 In this chapter, Allison Zmuda issues a challenge to school library media specialists (SLMSs) to become leaders in the assessment and reform process. In many school districts, the SLMS often finds it difficult to gain the recognition as essential partner in schoolwide planning. The battle begins with a lack of individual teacher cooperation and extends to administrative blindness. The opportunity to participate in the dynamic discussion of curricular adjustments remains out of reach for far too many professional librarians. Zmuda offers a call to action that relies on proactive research with reliable results. Building data, taking it to discussion, and relentlessly preaching Information Literacy Standard correlations are a few of the methods presented here. Various planning documents are included to give all of us the grounding necessary to pursue success.

Where Does Your Authority Come From?

Summary of the Sunday General Session at the AASL Fall Forum

Author's Note: This article is based on a keynote address delivered at the 2006 Fall Forum sponsored by the American Association of School Librarians in Providence, Rhode Island.

This session was anchored around the assertion that true authority does not come from the superintendent, principal, or even the teachers worked with every day; it comes from a very large achievement gap. The chasm between the academic expectations and the current achievement levels of students within the school creates the urgency and authority needed for school library media specialists (SLMSs) to work directly with students on tasks of significance.

Although SLMSs have worked diligently for years to collaborate with classroom teachers in their buildings, the power of those collaborations has largely been defined by the personalities and pedagogies of their colleagues. The quality of the instructional design, the relevance and rigor of the student task, and the determination of the strength of the performance are all owned by the classroom teacher. Any sharing of that responsibility is based on the graciousness of the teacher, not the authority, competence, or capacity of the SLMS. This limited form of collaboration relegates the SLMS to a supportive rather than collegial role.

The job of the SLMS is not to cover information literacy content, to leave it in the hands of classroom teachers to evaluate student achievement in information literacy, or to only work with the students who come through the library media center doors. The SLMS's job is to prepare students to be successful for the twenty-first-century world as defined by their individual school mission statements and local, state, and national standards in information literacy and technology. To accomplish these academic expectations, SLMSs must not only embed these goals in curriculum and instructional experiences but must evaluate the degree to which students have been successful at attaining the goals. This necessitates the design of rigorous, authentic tasks where students are required to transfer what they have learned

Allison Zmuda
Senior Education Specialist, Capitol Regional Education Council (CREC), Hartford, Connecticut

to new situations. These tasks should be measured by a standard rubric that encompasses both the subject area content from the classroom teacher and the information literacy development from the SLMS. For too long, SLMSs have participated in the process of the task but have not been ultimately privy to (or accountable for) the result of that effort. While grading students can be time consuming, it also is the only real way to gain access to data about whether the designed instructional experience had the intended achievement effect.

In order to claim this authority, SLMSs can adopt a basic improvement planning construct similar to one used by their superintendent or building principal. This particular model is grounded in five key moves as part of a larger recursive process:

1. **Clarify the vision and the goals.** Many SLMSs work, in good faith, on the wrong job. What role must the SLMS (and the school media center) play in the schooling of children if the system is to achieve its mission? This vision must be framed in language that is credible, relevant, and measurable so that it can be accomplished.

2. **Get credible evidence.** Without the data to illustrate achievement gaps, other staff and administrators perceive advocacy by SLMSs to be a rhetorical contention based on a biased viewpoint expressed by the professionals that seem to have the most to gain. What is the current achievement level of students in the area of information literacy and technology? What is the current data around library media usage? (Not just number of visits, but also the nature of the work completed during those visits.) It is critical to measure what is necessary, not just what is convenient. So it isn't enough to measure the number of students who came to the library media center in a month; the student learning that was accomplished also must be measured. What relationship is there between student attendance and quality of tasks completed in the library media center and their achievement on information literacy goals? (These goals are measured both in locally developed research tasks and embedded in questions on subject area standardized tests.)

3. **Assess the inevitable gap.** Gaps between current achievement levels and the established goals are the engine of school reform. By clearly defining the learning problems, the SLMS can work in concert with other staff to effectively marshal their resources, talents, and expertise to increase student learning. How should information be presented to administrators and teachers so that they can view the demand for more and better student work in the library media center as an achievement problem, not a personal preference?

4. **Plan actions to narrow/close the gap.** Coverage of content isn't enough—students must become accomplished in information literacy and technology. They must be able to transfer their learning to new and authentic challenges that they face not only in their classrooms but in the real world. What time, resources, and strategies do we need to accomplish our agreed-upon vision?

5. **Analyze results and act on feedback.** The success of the action plan is not measured on whether it was completed or not, but whether it had the intended effect on student learning. This requires a robust feedback system that provides the information needed about student work to reassess whether the achievement gap still exists. Did the action taken have the intended effect? What needs to happen next?

For more information about this cycle, refer to Wiggins and McTighe's *Schooling by Design* (ASCD, 2007) or Zmuda, Kuklis, and Kline's *Transforming Schools* (ASCD, 2004).

Ultimately, the heart of this reform effort requires full inclusion and partnership in the work of the school. The SLMS's authority to advocate for student achievement is already embedded in local mission statements, state and national standards, and standardized tests. The challenge now is to leverage what the system already has sworn it is committed to doing by becoming true partners with classroom teachers and school administrators in the name of student achievement.

Library Media Department Philosophy
Simsbury (Conn.) Public Schools

The goal of education is to give learners the opportunity to do something with what they know. A more rigorous and relevant form of accountability emerges when information is applied in search of a solution to a problem, to better understand a problem, or to create new knowledge. The foundation of our library media program is to facilitate the competence of learners as unique individuals with interests and ideas, citizens, and future members of the workforce. The development of that competence comes from the learner's clarity of task, ability to access information and literature, evaluate and synthesize information, produce critical and creative works, and communicate to an intended audience. Underlying this work is the learner's ability to critically think and problem solve in an efficient, effective, and ethical manner.

SLMSs design both stand-alone and collaborative learning experiences to provide all students with the opportunity to achieve the goals articulated in the Connecticut State Department of Education's Information and Technology Literacy Framework. The success of all students, however, depends upon the quality and consistency of the collaboration between the library media center and the classroom. SLMSs dedicate their professional efforts not only to ensure vital media and tools are available to students and staff but to ensure that students and staff make the use of these media and tools an integrated and meaningful part of teaching and learning.

Appendix A. Drafting a Curriculum Unit for Selecting Relevant Information: Grand Island (Neb.) Public Schools GIPS Standards

Big Six Skill 4—Use of Information Technology 5.0—Research 　　　　5.2—Electronic Resources	

Big Ideas (Enduring Understandings)	Essential Questions
Relevance of information is dependent on the purpose of the task and the perspective of the researcher.	Is this information useful?

Knowledge and Skills

K–2	3–5	6–8	9–12
Identify useful facts (GIPS Med. 4.1.1) Extract relevant information (GIPS Med. 4.2, Tech. 5.2.5)	Identify useful facts (GIPS Med. 4.1.1) Extract relevant information (GIPS Med. 4.2, Tech. 5.2.5)	Identify useful facts (GIPS Med. 4.1.1) Extract relevant information (GIPS Med. 4.2, Tech. 5.2.5)	Identify useful facts (GIPS Med. 4.1.1) Extract relevant information (GIPS Med. 4.2, Tech. 5.2.5)

Possible Assessment Ideas

Example: Given a nonfiction source and a set of research questions, students will highlight useful facts and relevant information.

Your ideas:

Appendix B. Nature of Teacher/SLMS Collaboration

Excerpted from A. Zmuda, "Where Does Your Authority Come From?" *School Library Media Activities Monthly* 23, no. 1 (2006): 19–22.

	Isolated Event	Coordinated Effort	Partnership
Design	Teacher approaches SLMS to reserve space in the library for students to complete a task using resources.	Teacher solicits information or ideas about what resources are available to support student work for the assigned task.	Teacher comes to SLMS with an idea for a research task or with a topic and works with the SLMS to further develop the idea.
Execution of Instruction	Teacher supervises student work in the library media center. SLMS provides class with a basic orientation of available resources (if appropriate) and may have made a list of relevant resources if given enough lead time. Teacher and students ask for assistance from the SLMS as questions or problems arise.	Teacher and SLMS provide support to students during the completion of the task: teacher primarily on the task parameters and grading expectations, SLMS primarily on how to access and use resources.	Teachers and SLMS each provide support to students during the completion of all aspects of the task: orienting them to the resources at hand; supporting their use of the resources and efforts to collect, analyze, and synthesize information; and clarifying task parameters and grading expectations.
Evaluation of Student Work	Teacher evaluates student work. Task parameters and grading expectations may or may not have been shared with the SLMS in advance.	Teacher evaluates student work (the grading expectations were shared with the SLMS prior to the students' work in the library media center).	Teacher and SLMS score student work together using a common rubric that includes criteria within both the teacher's content area and information literacy.
Reflection and Next Steps	SLMS waits to find out how it went—receives anecdotal information from teacher or student(s), but does not see student work or analysis of student achievement.	Teacher shares information with SLMS on how it went. May submit a sample of student work or a copy of the task for the SLMS's binder. Next steps are reserved until the teacher has another task in mind that requires the SLMS's support.	Based on student achievement on the task, teacher and SLMS draw conclusions about what the next task(s) should focus on to meet academic expectations within both teacher's content area and information literacy.

Collaboration Tracking Sheet			
MONTH of:	Isolated Event	Coordinated Effort	Partnership
Design			
Execution of Instruction			
Evaluation of Student Work			
Reflection and Next Steps			

AASL Information Literacy Standards for Student Learning Tracking Sheet			
	Indicators	Assessment Vehicles	Feedback System
Standard 1: The student who is information literate accesses information efficiently and effectively.			
Standard 2: The student who is information literate evaluates information critically and competently			
Standard 3: The student who is information literate uses information accurately and creatively.			
Standard 4: The student who is an independent learner is information literate and pursues information related to personal interests.			
Standard 5: The student who is an independent learner is information literate and appreciates literature and other creative expressions of information.			

Standard 6: The student who is an independent learner is information literate and strives for excellence in information seeking and knowledge generation.			
Standard 7: The student who contributes positively to the learning community and to society is information literate and recognizes the importance of information to a democratic society.			
Standard 8: The student who contributes positively to the learning community and to society is information literate and practices ethical behavior in regard to information and information technology.			
Standard 9: The student who contributes positively to the learning community and to society is information literate and participates effectively in groups to pursue and generate information.			

Voices of the Participants: Assessment and Advocacy

During the Fall Forum, audience members were asked to submit questions for evaluations and for inclusion in a continuing discussion via a newly developed ALA online community. Included here are some of the most significant questions posed by national institute participants with answers generated by the Teaching for Learning Committee.

When are teacher preparation and administrative certification classes going to incorporate information about the importance of media specialists and media centers?

I strongly believe that this information should be included in principal and teacher preparation programs, yet the research shows that it is not.

Hartzell, G. 2002. "The Principal's Perceptions of School Libraries and Teacher-librarians." *School Libraries Worldwide* 8, no. 1: 92–110.

Hartzell, G. (2002). *White House Conference on School Libraries: What's It Take?* <http://www.imls.gov/pubs/whitehouse0602/garyhartzell.htm>.

Wilson, P. J., and M. Blake. 1993. "The Missing Piece: A School Library Media Center Component in Principal-preparation Programs." *Record in Educational Leadership* 12, no. 2: 65–68.

Wilson, P. P., and A. J. MacNeil. 1998. "In the Dark: What's Keeping Principals from Understanding Libraries?" *School Library Journal* 44, no. 9: 114–16.

At Longwood University in Farmville, Virginia, our school library media faculty members visit teacher preparation classes to discuss the collaborative roles of the library media specialists in today's schools. We speak to our outgoing student teachers each semester to remind them to make an early connection to the library of their school. We speak to the student education association, which is the organization on campus for future teachers. Last semester, our library administration course partnered with a principal preparation course, providing online discussion forums for library issues in schools: future library media specialists and future principals reacted to and discussed various situations and scenarios.

What do we do with the assessment information once we have it? The class is done and won't likely return.

It depends on what type of assessment information you have collected.

Share it, as appropriate, with the classroom teacher. Perhaps he or she can use it to build upon skills in classroom instruction.

If appropriate, share it with the administration as evidence that the library makes a difference in student learning. You have collected the data. Of course, you would respect student privacy and confidentiality, but use the aggregated data to show that you are impacting student learning. You may also be able to use the data to show a need for more library resources in a particular subject area or at a particular grade level.—*Audrey Church, 2007 Teaching for Learning member*

We have *mandated*, year-long staff-development sessions during "planning" or after school. These can be valuable, *but* how do I *convince* my staff and administrator [*morale*] to do this in their plannings? Even though it's good, they are tired of being told what to do, or have to do.

This is time to work backwards. Find a class project that is working well and note the skill in use and a simple checklist that could be incorporated for assessment purposes. Teachers are tired of getting additional tasks. Your best strategy will be to help define and credit efforts already in place. Both Vi Harada and Marjorie Pappas have examples of useful charts included in this booklet. Once your teachers can refer to frameworks already in place, they may find it easier to cooperate with you in collecting useful data.—*Anita L. Vance, 2007 Teaching for Learning chair*

How can collaboration between the SLMS and classroom teacher be promoted by administration?

A few suggestions to offer when conferencing with administration to promote your School Library Program could include: During observations, some principals purposely plan a visit to the library during a team teaching event. The skill application process gets its best review within this setting, with both teacher and librarian sharing in the evaluative results. In many schools, time is allotted for librarians to announce new products and materials during faculty meetings. Working with Curriculum Directors for Act 48 hours, professional development sessions delivered by librarians heighten the overall support of the school district. New teacher orientation guidelines could offer library orientation as a mandated event.—*Anita L. Vance, 2007 Teaching for Learning chair*

How do we help/nudge the classroom teachers to value the process of information literacy/fluency more than the product? I am often so enthusiastic about working with teachers that I am accused of "badgering"—I'd like to have some tools to "make my case" that wouldn't be misperceived.

Give them data! In our data-driven educational environment, show them the numbers. Active involvement of the library media specialist in instruction positively impacts student achievement. You are not badgering to be badgering. You know that what you do makes a difference!

Studies completed by Keith Curry Lance, Marcia Rodney, and colleagues Donna Baumbach, James Baughman, Robert Burgin, Pamela Bracy, Dan Callison, Ross Todd, and Carol Kuhlthau show that what we do makes a difference in student learning. For information take a look at Scholastic's *School Libraries Work!* <http://www.scholastic.com/librarians/printables/downloads/slw_2006.pdf> and at the Library Research Service's School Library Impact Studies link <http://www.lrs.org/impact.asp>.

You can summarize the data found there: share statistics by preparing a library fast facts sheet, by including a statistic or two in the signature file of your email or on library bookmarks or on the daily announcements/bulletin. It shouldn't be overwhelming . . . just steady, measured doses.

Assessment Glossary

artifacts	Individual items produced by students and that provide evidence of learning.
assessment	The process of gathering evidence and documenting a student's learning and growth.
authentic assessment	Assessment that occurs as a regular part of instruction and in a real-life context.
bias	Systematic error introduced into sampling or testing by selecting or encouraging one outcome or answer over others.
content standards	Statements of what we want students to know and be able to do.
criterion-referenced test	Student performance is compared to a desired level of performance on the content. Questions on the assessment are selected to cover important content.
diagnostic assessment	Assessments conducted at the beginning of a unit or course to determine the present level of students' knowledge, skills, interests, and attitudes.
extended written response	Assessment requiring students to construct a written answer in response to a question or task rather than select one from a list.
formative assessment	Assessments conducted periodically throughout instruction to monitor progress and provide feedback. Its intention is to facilitate or form learning.
grade equivalent score	Average score obtained by students in various grade levels. Scores are norm-referenced and go from K.0 to 12.9.
mastery scores	A statement of levels of proficiency on an assessment. Scores go from "way below competence" to "advanced competence" or similar terminology. This is a criterion-referenced score.
norm-referenced test	Student performance is compared to that of other students to identify relative standing. Questions on the assessment are selected to cover important content as well as to "spread" students out on a continuum of achievement so that relative standing can be determined.
percent correct score	Number of points scored divided by number possible. A criterion-referenced score from 0 to 100.
percentile score	The percent of students scoring at or below a given score. A norm-referenced score going from 1 to 99.
performance assessment	Assessment based on observation and judgment looking at the quality of the performance or product.
performance standards	Statements that relate level of performance on an assessment to various levels of proficiency.
personal communication	Gathering information about student learning through communications such as journals and logs, interviews or conferences, and oral participation.
portfolio	A selection of a student's work compiled over a period of time and used for assessing performance or progress
raw score	Total number of points scored on an assessment. Scores go from 0 to total possible.
rubric	A scoring grid designed to identify criteria for successful performance and describe the different levels of performance.
selected response	Assessments in which students select the correct or best response from the list provided.

standardized	Assessment and scoring procedures are uniform. Students take the test at the same time in the same way so that results can be compared across test takers.
standards-based assessment	Student performance is compared to a desired level of performance on the content. Questions on the assessment are selected to cover important content and/or match state or local content standards.
stanine scores	Broad indicator of student standing in relationship to other students. This is a norm-referenced score ranging from 1 to 9.
summative assessment	Assessments conducted at the end of an instructional unit or semester to judge the final quality and quantity of student achievement, the success of the instructional program, or both. They sum up performance and provide the data for giving grades. The judgments about student achievement are communicated to interested audiences.

References

American Association of School Librarians and Association for Educational Communications and Technology. *Information Power: Building Partnerships for Learning.* Chicago: ALA, 1998.

Andrade, H. G. 2000. "Using Rubrics to Promote Thinking and Learning." *Educational Leadership* 57, no. 5 (2000): 13–18.

Asp, E. "The Relationship between Large-scale and Classroom Assessment: Compatibility or Conflict?" In *Assessing Student Learning: New Rules, New Realities*, 17–46, ed. R. Brandt. Arlington, Va.: Educational Research Service, 1998.

Bilal, D. "Children's Use of the Yahooligans! Web Search Engine I: Cognitive, Physical, and Affective Behaviors on Fact-based Search Tasks." *Journal of the American Society for Information Science and Technology* 58, no. 7 (2000): 646–65.

Black, P., and D. William. "Inside the Black Box: Raising Standards through Assessment." *Phi Delta Kappan* 80, no. 2 (1998): 139–47.

Bransford, J., A. L. Brown, and R. R. Cocking, eds. *How People Learn: Brain, Mind, Experience, and School.* Washington D.C.: National Academy Pr., 2002.

Cawelti, G., ed. *Handbook of Research on Improving Student Achievement,* 3d ed. Arlington, Va.: Educational Research Service, 2004.

Chappuis, J., and R. J. Stiggins. "Classroom Assessment for Learning." *Educational Leadership* 60, no. 1 (2002): 40–43.

Chi, M. T. H. "Self-explaining: The Dual Processes of Generating Inference and Repairing Mental Models." In *Advances in Instruction Psychology,* 161–238, ed. R. Glaser. Mahwah, N.J.: Erlbaum, 2000.

Coatney, S. "Assessment for Learning." In *Curriculum Connections throughout the Library,* 157–68, ed. B. K. Stripling and S. Hughes-Hassell. Westport, Conn.: Libraries Unlimited, 2003.

Cross, K. P. *Learning Is about Making Connections.* Princeton, N.J.: Educational Testing Service, 1999.

Davies, A. *Making Classroom Assessment Work.* Courtenay, B.C.: Connections, 2000.

Davies, A., et al. *Together Is Better: Collaborative Assessment, Evaluation, and Reporting.* Winnipeg: Portage and Main Pr., 1992.

Dembo, M. H., and M. J. Eaton. "Self-regulation of Academic Learning in Middle-level Schools." *The Elementary School Journal* 100, no. 5 (2000): 472–90.

Dickinson, G. "How One Child Learns: The Teacher-librarian As Evidence-based Practitioner." *Teacher Librarian* 33, no. 1 (2005): 16–20.

Donham, J. *Assessment of Information Processes and Products.* McHenry, Ill.: Follett Software Co., 1998.

Earl, L. M. *Assessment As Learning: Using Classroom Assessment to Maximize Student Learning.* Thousand Oaks, Calif.: Corwin Pr., 2003.

Ekhaml, L. "Graphic Organizers: Outlets for Your Thoughts." *School Library Media Activities Monthly* 14, no. 5 (1998): 29–33.

Elmore, R. F. *School Reform from the Inside Out: Policy, Practice, and Performance.* Cambridge, Mass.: Harvard Education Pr., 2004.

Ericson, K. A. "Attaining Excellence through Deliberate Practice: Insights from the Study of Expert Performance." In *The Pursuit of Excellence in Education,* 21–55, ed. M. Ferrari. Hillsdale, N.J.: Erlbaum, 2002.

Falk, B. *The Heart of the Matter: Using Standards and Assessment to Learn.* Portsmouth, N.H.: Heinemann, 2000.

Farmer, S. J. *Student Success and Library Media Programs: A Systems Approach to Research and Best Practice.* Westport, Conn.: Libraries Unlimited, 2003.

Fidel, R. D., et al., "A Visit to the Information Mall: Web Searching Behavior of High School Students." *Journal of the American Society for Information Science* 50, no. 1 (1999): 24–37.

Fitzgerald, M. A. "Evaluating Information: An Information Literacy Challenge." *School Library Media Research* 2 (1999). <http://www.ala.org/ala/aasl/aaslpubsandjournals/slmrb/slmrcontents/volume21999/vol2fitzgerald.htm>.

Garland, K. "The Information Search Process: A Study of Elements Associated with Meaningful Research Tasks." *School Libraries Worldwide* 1, no. 1 (1995): 41–53.

Gordon, C., "The Effects of Concept Mapping on the Searching Behavior of Tenth-grade Students." *School Library Media Research* 3 (2000). <http://www.ala.org/ala/aasl/aaslpubsandjournals/clmrb/clmrcontents/volume3200/mapping.htm>.

Gusky, T. R. "How Classroom Assessments Improve Learning." *Educational Leadership* 60, no. 5 (2003): 6–11.

Harada, V. H., "Personalizing the Information Search Process: A Case Study of Journal Writing with Elementary-age Students." *School Library Media Research* 5 (2002). <http://www.ala.org/aaslpubsand journals/slmrb/slmrcontents/volume52002/harada.htm>.

Harada V. H. "Working Smarter: Being Strategic about Assessment and Accountability." T*eacher Librarian* 33, no. 1 (2005): 8–15.

Harada V. H., D. Lum, and K. Sooza. "Building a Learning Community: Students and Adults As Inquirers." *Childhood Education* 79, no. 2 (2002/2003): 66–71.

Harada, V. H., and J. M. Yoshina. *Assessing Learning: Librarians and Teachers As Partners.* Westport, Conn.: Libraries Unlimited, 2005.

Harada, V. H., and J. M. Yoshima. "Assessing Learning: The Missing Piece in Instruction?" *School Library Media Activities Monthly* 22, no. 7 (2006): 20–23.

Hawley, W. D., and D. I. Rollie. *The Keys to Effective Schools: Educational Reform As Continuous Improvement.* Thousand Oaks, Calif.: Corwin Pr., 2002.

Herman J. L., P. R. Aschbacker, and L. Winters. *A Practical Guide to Alternative Assessment.* Alexandria, Va.: Association for Supervision and Alexandria Curriculum Development, 1992.

Knechlin, C., and S. Zwann. *Build Your Own Information Literate School.* Salt Lake City: Hi Willow, 2003.

Kuhlthau. C. C., ed. *Information Literacy: Learning How to Learn.* Chicago: ALA, 1991.

Kuhlthau. C. C., ed. *Assessment and the School Library Media Center.* Edgewood, Colo.: Libraries Unlimited, 1992.

Kuhlthau. C. C., ed. *Seeking Meaning: A Process Approach to Library and Information Services.* Norwood, N.J.: Ablex, 1993.

Linn, R. J. "Complex Performance-based Assessment: Expectations and Validations Criteria." *Educational Researcher* 20, no. 8 (1991): 15–21.

Loertscher, D. V., and K. Lance. *Powering Achievement: School Library Media Programs Make a Difference: The Evidence,* 2nd ed. San Jose, Calif.: Hi Willow, 2002.

Loertscher, D. V., and B. Woolls, eds. *Information Literacy: A Review of the Research,* 2d ed. San Jose, Calif.: Hi Willow, 2002.

Loertscher, D.V., with R.Todd, *We Boost Achievement! Evidence-based Practice for School Library Media Centers.* Salt Lake City: Hi Willow, 2003.

Martin-Kniep, G. "Reflection: A Key to Developing Greater Self-understanding." In *Becoming a Better Teacher: Eight Innovations That Work.* Alexandria, Va.: Association for Supervision and Curriculum Development, 2000.

Marzano, R. J., D. Pickering, and J. McTighe. *Assessing Student Outcomes: Performance Assessment Using the Dimensions of Learning Model.* Alexandria, Va.: Association for Supervision and Curriculum Development, 1993.

Marzano, R. J. *What Works in Schools: Translating Research into Action.* Alexandria, Va.: Association for Supervision and Curriculum Development, 2003.

McGregor, J., and D. C. Streitenberger. "Do Scribes Learn? Copying and Information Use." *School Library Media Research* 1 (1998). <http://www.ala.org/ala/aasl/aaslpubsandjournals/slmrb/slmrcontents/volume11998slmqo/mcgregor.cfm>.

Neuman, D. "Information Power and Assessment: The Other Side of the Standards Coin." In *Educational Media and Technology Yearbook,* 110–19, ed. R. M. Branch and M. A. Fitzgerald. Englewood, Colo.: Libraries Unlimited, 2000.

Newell, T. S. "Thinking Beyond the Disjunctive Opposition of Information Literacy Assessment in Theory and Practice." *School Library Media Research* 7 (2004). <http://www.ala.org/ala/aasl/aaslpubsandjournals/slmrb/slmrcontents/volume72004/beyond.htm>.

North Central Regional Educational Laboratory. 21st Century Skills. <http://www.ncrel.org.enguage/skills/agelit.htm>.

Northwest Regional Educational Laboratory. Assessment Home—Toolkit98 (2001). <http://nwrel.org/assessment/toolkit98.php>.

O'Callaghan, W. G. *Thinking Outside the Box: How Educational Leaders Can Safely Navigate through the Rough Waters of Change.* Lanham, Md.: Scarecrow, 2004.

Pappas, M. "Organizing Research." *School Library Media Activities Monthly* 14, no. 4 (1997): 30–32.

Pearson Prentice Hall. Professional Development, Hot Topics, Assessment (2006). <http://www.phschool.com/professional_development/assessment/rubrics.html>.

Schrock, K. *Kathy Schrock's Guide for Educators: Assessment and Rubric Information* (2006). <http://school.discovery.com/schrockguide/assess.html>.

Stefl-Mahry, J. "Building Rubrics into Powerful Learning Assessment Tools." *Knowledge Quest* 32, no. 5 (2003): 19–23.

Stiggins, R. J. "The Assessment Crisis: The Absence of Assessment FOR Learning." *Phi Delta Kappan* 83, no. 10 (2002): 758–765.

Stiggins, R. J. *Student-involved Assessment for Learning,* 4th ed. Upper Saddle River, N.J.: Pearson/Merrill Prentice Hall, 2005.

Strickland, K., and J. Strickland. *Making Assessment Elementary.* Portsmouth, N.H.: Heinemann, 2000.

Stripling, B. K. "Expectations for Achievement and Performance: Assessing Student Skills." *NASSP Bulletin* 83, no. 605 (1999): 44–52.

Todd, R. J. 2002. "Evidence-based Practice: The Sustainable Future for Teacher-librarians." *SCAN* 21, no. 1 (2002): 30–37. <http://www.schools.nsw.edu.au/schoollibraries/scan/researchfeature.htm>.

Todd. R. J. 2002. "Evidence-based Practice II: Getting into the Action." *SCAN* 21, no. 2 (2002): 34–41. <http://www.schools.nsw.edu.au/schoollibraries/scan/researchfeature.htm>.

Todd, R. J. "School Libraries Evidence: Seize the Day, Begin the Future." *Library Media Connection* 22, no. 1 (2003): 12–17.

University of Kansas Center for Research on Learning. "Rubistar: Create Rubrics for Our Project-based Learning Activities" (2006). <http://rubistar.4teachers.org/index.php>.

University of Wisconsin–Stout. "Rubrics: Teacher Created Rubrics for Assessment" (2006). <http://www.uwstout.edu/soe/profedev/rubrics.shtml>.

Wagner, T. *Making The Grade: Reinvesting in America's Schools.* New York: Routledge Falmer, 1997.

Wiggins, G. *Educative Assessment: Designing Assessments to Inform and Improve Student Performance.* San Francisco: Jossey-Bass, 1998.

Wiggins, G., and J. McTighe. *Understanding by Design.* Alexandria, Va.: Association for Supervision and Curriculum Development, 1998.

Wiggins, G., and J. McTighe. *Understanding by Design,* 2nd ed. Alexandria, Va.: Association for Supervision and Curriculum Development, 2006.

William, D. C., et al. "Teachers Developing Assessment for Learning: Impact on Student Achievement." *Assessment in Education: Principles, Policy, and Practice* 11, no. 1 (2004): 49–65.

Wiske, M. S. "How Teaching for Understanding Changes the Rules in the Classroom." *Educational Leadership* 51, no. 5 (1994): 19–21.

Zmuda, A., R. Kuklis, and K. Kline. *Transforming Schools.* Alexandria, Va.: Association for Supervision of Curriculum and Development, 2004.

Zmuda, A. "Where Does Your Authority Come from? Empowering the Library Media Specialist As a True Partner in Student Achievement." *School Library Media Activities Monthly* 23, no. 1 (2006): 19–22.

In Search of Testing and Test Anxiety Fiction

By Cathie Marriott

It was an arduous, anxiety-ridden search that covered almost two years. The Teaching for Learning Committee, with the support of AASL leadership, agreed that the topic for the 2006 Fall Forum would be assessment. At that 2004 Midwinter Meeting, it was decided that we locate books that deal with anxiety, specifically school and test anxiety. The committee members hit the exhibit floor with the goal of locating these books. We could find some excellent nonfiction books that dealt with stress; however, our goal was to include fiction. We all knew such books as Judy Finchler's *Testing Mrs. Malarkey* (Walker and Co., 2000) and Kathryn Cave's *You've Got Dragons* (Peachtree, 2003). These titles identified anxieties, taught readers how to manage them, and chased these anxieties away. Anxiety associated with report cards, another form of standardized assessment, caused concerns for Hank in Henry Winkler's *I Got a D in Salami* (Grosset and Dunlop, 2006). Additional titles cover the broader scope of various types of school assessments. This bibliography links a variety of perspectives with the Fall Forum participants as we all work together to identify assessments, learn how to manage them, and chase away our own anxieties.

Testing and Test Anxiety Fiction: A Selected Bibliography

Grades K–3

Brown, Marc. *Arthur and the True Francine.* Little, Brown, 1996.
　　Francine and Muffy are good friends until Muffy lets Francine take the blame for cheating on a test.
Berenstain, Stan. *The Berenstain Bears' Report Card Troubles.* Random House, 2002.
　　When Brother Bear spends too much time on sports and brings home a terrible report card, the whole family pitches in to help him improve his grades.
Cave, Kathryn. *You've Got Dragons.* Peachtree, 2003.
　　A boy deals with his dragons by getting to know them, talking to others about them, and learning that they do go away.
Cohen, Miriam. *First Grade Takes a Test.* Greenwillow Books, 1980.
　　The first grade is distressed by an intelligence test that fails to measure true aptitude.
Finchler, Judy. *Testing Miss Malarkey.* Walker and Co., 2000.
　　Although the teachers, principal, and parents all say that "The Test" is not important, their actions tell another story.
Flood, Pansie Hart. *It's Test Day, Tiger Turcotte.* CarolRhoda Books, 2004.
　　Already so worried about the big test that his stomach is upset, seven-year-old Tiger, whose parents are black, Meherrin Indian, and Hispanic, gets stuck on the question about race.

Giff, Patricia. *Lazy Lions, Lucky Lambs.* Delacorte Pr., 1985.

> Richard likes to draw but has a very hard time writing. He is in despair over a paper due just before report card time until his sister gives him a good idea.

Granowsky, Alvin. *Ronald's Report Card.* Modern Curriculum Pr., 1986.

> Ronald is doing better in school, but is disappointed when a computer mistake causes his report card to show low grades.

Garvey, Linda K., Danny Campbell, and Kimberly Campbell. *Doug Cheats.* Disney, 1999.

> Knowing that Doug wants to do well on an upcoming history test to impress the girl of his dreams, Roger tempts him with a copy of the test.

Havill, Juanita. *Jamaica and the Substitute Teacher.* Houghton Mifflin, 1999.

> Jamaica copies from a friend during a spelling test because she wants a perfect paper, but her substitute teacher, Mrs. Duvall, helps her understand that she doesn't have to be perfect to be special.

Huelin, Jodi. *Rainbow Fish: Don't Cheat, Rusty!* Harper Festival, 2003.

> Rusty is afraid that Miss Cuttle will he disappointed if he fails the big test on seashells.

Park, Barbara. *Junie B. Jones, First Grader: Cheater Pants.* Random House, 2003.

> Junie B. Jones knows all about cheating—it's wrong! But what about copying someone else's homework? Is sharing the same as cheating?

Poydar, Nancy. *The Biggest Test in the Universe.* Holiday House, 2005.

> Sam is getting nervous. The BIG TEST is coming! That's what all the kids say. Are they telling the truth?

Rosenberry, Vera. *Vera Runs Away.* Henry Holt, 2000.

> When her family seems too busy to appreciate her good report card, first-grader Vera decides to find somewhere else to live.

Simmons, Alex. *Grounded for Life?* Troll Associates, 1994.

> Afraid he will have to drop out of karate class if his math grades don't improve, Matthew is tempted to cheat on a big test.

Thaler, Mike. *The Bully Brothers Make the Grade.* Scholastic, 1995.

> The Bully Brothers are straight-A students. NOT! They have been changing grades on their report cards. What are they going to do when their mother is invited to school for parent-teacher night?

Grades 3–6

Avi. *The Secret School.* Harcourt, 2002.

> In 1925, fourteen-year-old Ida Bidson takes over as teacher when the one-room schoolhouse closes unexpectedly.

Bosch, Carl W. *Making the Grade.* Parenting Pr., 1991.

> You, the reader, decide what to do when you receive a bad report card because of the extra soccer practice you've been doing. Do you tell your parents, or try to keep it a secret?

Dubowski, Cathy East. *My Fourth-Grade Mess.* Minstrel, 1996.

> The teacher says that Michelle cheated on a test—but she didn't.

Levy, Elizabeth. *Cheater, Cheater.* Scholastic, 1993.

> When Lucy enters junior high school, she finds out the hard way that putting herself on the line to impress new friends is a bad idea and can lead to suspension from school.

Peters, Julie Anne. *How Do You Spell Geek?* Avon, 1996.

> The relationship between best friends Kimberly and Ann is put to the test when Ann takes a geeky new student under her wing and encourages her to compete against front-runner Kimberly in a spelling bee.

Winkler, Henry, and Lin Oliver. *I Got a D in Salami.* Grosset & Dunlap, 2006.

> Problems arise after Hank throws his report card in a meat grinder.

Grades 4–7

Clements, Andrew. *The Report Card.* Simon & Schuster, 2004.

> Fifth-grader Nora Rowley has always hidden the fact that she's a genius from everyone because all she wants is to be normal. However, when she comes up with a plan to prove that grades are not important, things begin to get out of control.

Korman, Gordon. *The 6th Grade Nickname Game.* Hyperion, 1998.

> The substitute sixth-grade teacher is in danger of losing his job if the class does not do well on the state test.

Pierce, Tamora. *First Test.* Random House, 2005.

> This is the first in a series featuring the wonderful character Keladry of Mindelan, the first girl to take advantage of a decree that permits girls to train for knighthood.

Grades 5–9

Day, Lauren. *What Kind of Friend Are You?* Scholastic, 1999.

> Somebody's cheating off Rocket.

Koss, Amy Goldman. *The Cheat.* Dial Books, 2003.

> When Sarah gets her hands on the answers to the eighth-grade geography midterm and decides to share them with some other students, the consequences are far-ranging.

Young Adult

Capp, Nan Willard. *Cheating Lessons: A Novel.* Atheneum Books, 2002.

> When her team is announced as finalists in the State Classics Bowl, Bernadette suspects that cheating might have been involved.

Fogelin, Adrian. *The Real Question.* Peachtree, 2006.

> Sixteen-year-old Fisher Brown decides to stop cramming for the SATs and accompanies his homeless neighbor on an out-of-town roof repair job.

Fredericks, Mariah. *Crunch Time.* Simon & Schuster, 2006.

> Four students form a study group to improve their SAT scores. Will that be enough?

Harrison, Lisa. *Best Friends for Never: A Clique Novel.* Little, Brown, 2004.

> A bet about wardrobes between the wealthy Massie and middle class Claire results in a testing of old friendships, a forging of new ones, and a change for the student body at Octavian Country Day School.

Keene, Carolyn. *Cheating Hearts.* Pocket, 1990.

> School newspaper editor Karen Jacob's discovery of a cheating ring at River Heights High School threatens her romance with popular Ben Newhouse, while Nikki Masters finds herself torn between two boys—British newcomer Niles Butler and old flame Tim Cooper.

Levithan, David. *The Perfect Score.* Simon Spotlight, 2004.

Six high school seniors from diverse backgrounds decide that the only way they're going to ace the SAT is to steal the answers.

Roos, Stephen. *Confessions of a Wayward Preppie.* Delacorte Pr., 1986.

During his first year at an exclusive prep school, Cary is caught in a campaign of hatred between his two roommates and faces the temptation to help a friend cheat.

Speregen, Devra Newberger. *To Cheat or Not to Cheat.* Minstrel Books, 1998.

Getting a study sheet from her friend Lara, Stephanie is unaware that it is a copy of that year's test, which her friend has swiped from the teacher's desk.

Steele, J. M. *The Taker.* Hyperion, 2006.

Carly's future looks great—grades are good, captain of the lacrosse team, the best boyfriend, and a shoo-in for Princeton—until she tanks the SAT. How far will she go to get a better score?

Yee, Lisa. *Stanford Wong Flunks Big Time.* Arthur Levine Books/Scholastic, 2005.

The star of the basketball team fails English and must give up the opportunity to attend a prestigious summer basketball camp—and tries to keep it a secret from his friends.